Professor Carol's

Why Freshmen Fail
and how to avoid it.

Plus
Tips for Flourishing in College

by Carol B. Reynolds, Ph.D.

Illustrations by Paul Bass
Edited by Jane M. Elder

Silver Age Music
Plano, Texas

Published in the United States by Silver Age Music, Inc.

Plano, Texas U.S.A.

Professor Carol is a registered trademark of
Silver Age Music, Inc.

ISBN 978-0-9819990-7-4

Carol B. Reynolds, author
Paul Bass, illustrator
Why Freshmen Fail
and how to avoid it.
Plus Tips for Flourishing in College
First U.S. Edition

Copyright 2016 by Silver Age Music, Inc.
All rights reserved under International and Pan-American Copyright Conventions. No part of this boook may be reproduced or transmitted in any form by any means, electronic or mechanical, including photocopying, recording, or by any information storage and retrieval system, without permission in writing from the Publisher.

Printed in the United States of America

Table of Contents

PART I: WHY FRESHMEN FAIL v

Introduction vii

1. My Own Story 1
2. They're Off! 7
3. Why Am I Here? 11
4. Too Much 19
5. Alone in the Crowd 23
6. Real Life 29
7. The ABCs 37
8. "Free" Time 47
9. Who Is the Teacher? 53
10. Where Do I Need To Be Right Now? 65

PART II: TIPS FOR FLOURISHING IN COLLEGE 73

11. The Nod Factor 75
12. What NOT To Ask 81
13. The Adventure of Office Hours 89
14. The "Who and What" Strategy 97
15. What Not To Say 105
16. The Good News about Today's Colleges 113
17. Are They Really Ready? 119

About the Author 127

PART I

Why Freshmen Fail

Introduction

I come to this topic honestly. My own freshman year back at Ohio University in 1969 was filled with mistakes and poor decisions, including several that I'll mention in the course of this book. Furthermore, it took me more than one attempt to "get college right." Suffice it to say, I bring personal experience in "failure" to the discussion.

In time, I righted my course and found the formulas I needed to excel. But later, in my career as a professor, I watched an annual parade of first-year students make the same mistakes I had made. The times surely have changed since I was a freshman, but the pitfalls facing first-year students have remained remarkably the same

In retirement, especially in my new role as "Professor Carol," I find myself giving frequent talks about college success to parents and students across the country. No matter where I am, my remarks trigger an outpouring of memories in my adult listeners—many of them bitter memories. Even if they themselves scraped out a decent first year at college, they likely watched friends, relatives, or roommates falter and fail.

High-school students who attend these talks register surprise at the negative comments they hear from adults who speak up during these sessions. "How can this be?" You almost see their eyes widening in disbelief. "Wait, this is *college*—the very thing adults have been preparing me to undertake for my whole life." Understandably, these kids have been so focused on getting into college that there has been little time to consider what can go wrong. Furthermore, they cannot imagine their parents and teachers withering under the situations I describe in my talks.

Kids don't necessarily realize that most people who attended college recall at least one awful teacher whose mere name sends shudders up the spine! Common, too, are memories of classes that annoyed, disappointed, or angered. Young people can not imagine unfocused or baffling professors who rarely taught on topic, big introductory classes poorly run by overworked teaching assistants, unfair practices such as papers never returned and grades unfairly issued, or routine cancelling of classes necessary to complete a major.

Taken together, my discussion of these realities of college life may produce surprises, especially in young readers. In the first part of this book, I give the top eight reasons that students fail in college. The second part of the book is filled with advice that, without question, can help a student avoid many of the pitfalls that await first-year students in today's colleges, universities, and vocational schools. Throughout the pages, I emphasize the *real life* skills needed for a successful college experience. Such skills cannot be measured by transcripts and SAT scores.

One more thing. In light of the enormous expense of college today, students need to approach college with the most maturity possible. People are finally beginning to speak more openly about the crippling costs of today's college education. They question the contradiction between the time-honored ideal of a university education and the realities that hit the 21st-century student right in the face, starting with financial ruin. It says a great deal that the blood-red cover of the July 2016 issue of *Consumer Reports* bears the banner: *I Kind of Ruined My Life by Going to College*.

To avoid this sad, but increasingly common, result, a student needs to be both academically prepared and emotionally purposed—focused and mature—before walking into (or logging onto) that first expensive class. Even the student who seems fully prepared "on paper" will meet with great surprises that can derail the college experience. Let me tell you my story.

CHAPTER 1

My Own Story

My college experience began in the summer of 1969. I was venturing from the sleepy southern city of Roanoke, Virginia, onto the intensely political campus of a major "northern" university (Ohio University). My credentials for admission into the university were strong on paper. I had played a fine audition for acceptance into the Music Department and merited a good scholarship. But I could not have been more unprepared.

Probably there is no need to remind readers that 1969 was a tumultuous time on America's campuses. My parents did not want me going so far from home, nor to such a big school. They acquiesced only because I had a generous scholarship and would be studying piano with a well-known teacher. A promising pianist from a young age, I played at a high level, specializing in the piano music of Russian composer Sergei Prokofiev. This is what caught the scholarship committee's attention. Coming from a generation that venerated Van Cliburn, my profile seemed to promise strong musical success.

Amidst the preparation to go off to college, I recall no discussion of any of the "pitfalls" awaiting me. Books such as this did not exist, even though they surely would have been helpful. Plus, times were different back then. College was still affordable (especially with the kind of scholarship I had received). Student loans, when necessary, were a supplemental resource that could be recommended without reservation. A lot was still on the line financially, but not nearly as much as there is today.

Could I have analyzed my own (un)preparedness back then or the challenges which faced me? I doubt it. No one asked me whether I *wanted* to be taking this step, and if they had, I had a pat answer down. But when I look back on it, my mother already foresaw my failures. And since my educational success was the most important goal for her, my failures caused her, as well as my father, great sadness.

Remember, attending college back then was considered a special privilege and it was assumed that anyone admitted would do well. Chances to "go to college" weren't everywhere, as they seem to be today. "Better luck next time" was not a phrase likely to be uttered if someone faltered.

I write all of this, first, in order to offer encouragement. We don't really know how smooth or rocky our children's paths will be. Plus, what seems like utter failure at one point may end up as a temporary bump. Or, perhaps it is more of a ravine into which students will fall, but out of which they will climb. Kids are resilient at seventeen, eighteen, or nineteen (just as they were as babies).

In addition, we do live in a country where it is common to make mistakes at this age and recover from them. A second chance (or third) would not be possible in many parts of the word, where educational opportunities are severely rationed and a failure is just that: a life-long failure.

But back to my own story. Of course, I *did* want to enter Ohio University. Nevertheless, my motives for wanting to be in college were far more tied up with wanting my "independence" and instant adulthood than with study and achievement. (I couldn't have voiced it, but someone questioning me deeply would have seen that to be true.)

Beyond that, I did not envision the level of practice and study that would be required (things had come too easily to me up to that point). Nor had I been around many performers of such high level before. I did not understand the rigors of competition. I did not know how to manage anything by myself (my dedicated mom had been the driving force behind my daily routine). Also, I fell prey to two of the biggest pitfalls you will read about in this book: 1) the inability to handle the deceptive freedom of the college class schedule and, 2) the practice of skipping classes that seemed common and so harmless.

It *wasn't* harmless. My failure to complete my freshmen year at Ohio University came about from these two reasons. This failure burned on my mind for many years: so many lost opportunities, especially considering the esteemed piano teacher I had.

Still, this was the U.S.A., and I was able to try again. After some time passed, I entered college again, also on a big scholarship, but this time at the North Carolina School of the Arts. It's embarrassing to admit that I had not fully reformed my attendance pattern, although I had come to terms with the need to treat each week as a continuum of practice and study, rather than an open playtime with a few academic interruptions.

At this school, I learned an enormous amount and had my first serious exposure to opera, ballet, and the life of the orchestral musician. But there were so many interesting artistic things going on at NCSA that I kept finding them more important than attending the classes I didn't like. I ended up with A's in most classes, but F's in others. I lasted only two semesters.

It is not pleasant to look back on these memories, although the decades in between have softened the edges. As a parent and grandparent, I feel most keenly how distressing my failures were to my parents, who had sacrificed for my education.

But no matter how much anyone sacrifices, it still comes down to the individual student making choices day by day: both big decisions (e.g., which school, what major, what classes) and small, seemingly innocuous ones (getting out of bed, spending an hour researching a paper rather than texting friends, etc.). You can get the big ones right but mishandle the small decisions and still fail.

It is these decisions that I hope to inform and affect within the text of this book. So let's get started.

Carol indeed graduates!

6 *Why Freshmen Fail*

CHAPTER 2

They're Off!

They're off, right? Finally!

It has taken eighteen years to get to the point where a nearly grown child is about to vault into the adult world. The destination may vary from a modest rural college to a huge urban university, a fast-paced vocational school, or a regimen of online classes: it does not matter. A new reality is coming.

If you are the student in this picture, you can almost smell the delicious aroma of independence. If you are the parent, you are about to watch your baby take an irreversible step into uncharted waters. No matter which part you play in this equation, it is a nervous time.

So what are the waters into which a first-year student will step? Parents and students have a mixed set of ideals to characterize the approaching venture. The parental ideal often incorporates snapshots of landscaped campuses and stately buildings, hushed library corridors and polished study desks. Students entertain some of that same imagery, for sure, but they anticipate far more the dorm life, new friendships, and the long-awaited chance to make their own choices free from mom or dad.

These idealized visions are both valid and full of holes. Polished desks, beautifully trimmed lawns and glitzy student centers with busy food courts will indeed greet the arriving families. And the parents must acknowledge (with a sinking feeling) that, within a matter of hours, no one, absolutely no one, will be monitoring any of their child's daily decisions.

But hovering above that set of facts, the realities of today's higher education system are not as "trimmed" as parents think. A college has far less polish, less focus on learning, and less accountability than the slick orientation material leads the incoming student to believe. If that sounds worrisome, it is.

College Has Changed

Before going further, we must recognize the major changes occurring in the American college system.

Throughout this book, I will frame my discussion in terms of the iconic view of "going to college," where a student lives in a dorm, takes classes in different buildings across a campus, seeks out professors during office hours, and associates with fellow students on campus. Many of the same points also apply to those students lucky enough to live at home, where mom may do their laundry, or at least give them access to a free machine!

Students increasingly enter college with a bundle of credits earned through dual-credit programs, AP and CLEP testing, and online courses taken while in high school. The wildfire-spread of online learning, a hugely positive factor in my view, is radically changing the dynamics of American campus life. For certain, the whole system may look different in a few years. We do not know how things will evolve.

Reconciling Two Visions

Now, let's return to the dual visions parents and students entertain, and think about those final days before a teen leaves for college. He or she rumbles around upstairs, ruffling through stacks of t-shirts and taking high-school treasures off the wall. The parents sit at the dining room table staring at the bank statement and consoling themselves with the belief that a traditional university education will provide the key to their child's future success in life. But it's hard to reconcile those visions, isn't it? The parent's ideal for college frequently clashes with the goals the kids have. Yes, teenagers will give lip service to the "idealized college-education," and they genuinely may be excited about it. But the real thing they're excited about is this:

they are off and on their own.

Parents, do you remember being seventeen? Eighteen? It hasn't been so very long ago for some of you reading this book. Think back: what did you want? Don't think too hard about it—it can frighten you to remember how you reasoned things out back then. But rest assured, most kids are thinking about one thing at this critical point: the chance to live out "on their own."

I know I was. I focused principally on a fantasized version of "independence," despite what I said to my family. Despite the marvelous music scholarship I mentioned in the introduction. Despite the exciting academic offerings that stood before me at Ohio University. All of that was abstract to me. I imagined only the freedom that would magically appear after kissing my parents goodbye and walking into a dorm.

This is, of course, the wonderful and terrifying truth about being eighteen. And that same youthful enthusiasm makes it hard for an 18-year-old to anticipate the tiny (and not so tiny) missteps that will derail the entire college venture. This drama will unfold not on a stage in a theater, but rather in a series of disconnected scenes in a young person's life.

So let's pull the curtain back and look at the first reason that causes freshmen to fail. We will start with the simplest reason you can imagine, yet one of the hardest to grasp and work with. They don't want to be there.

CHAPTER 3

Why Am I Here?

Yes, you read that right. They *don't* want to go to college. Oh, they want to go away from home, be independent, experience adult life, spread their wings and fly. And they expect to succeed: they did not go through all this preparation hoping to catapult to the ground. But actually doing what is necessary to obtain a college education, per se? That is a different matter entirely.

Let me pose a question to the parents: have you sat down with your kids and asked them to give you *two* reasons why they are going to college? I mean valid, real-life reasons. They know what to say, because they are not fools. But I want you to dig deeper.

Can they give you reasons that stand up to scrutiny? This will be a hard conversation and may be impossible for parents to conduct. The visions, motives, and dynamics between the child and parent easily get tangled. So maybe an uncle, a clergy member, or a close neighbor could have this conversation with them. "Why are you going to college?" "Why *really* are you doing this?"

Admittedly, I have posed a complex question. Adults sometimes find it difficult to answer similar questions: "Why are you *really* changing jobs?" "Why are you declining to serve on the Board, since you spend so much time with the organization?" "Why not admit that you need to downsize and move into a retirement community?" Pinpointing and justifying our motives is not so easy.

Sometimes, though, students will give a strong answer to the tough question, "Why are you going to college?" A teen determined to become a lawyer or a surgeon knows why he or she needs college. That does not mean things will necessarily work out. But that child can at least give a real reason.

Along those same lines, parents might hear, "Grandma, you know I *always* wanted to be a dentist like granddad." Or, "Aunt Miriam, I have dreamed of being a pilot ever since we flew to England, and you *know* that requires going to college!" These answers will show a child's clear focus towards something envisioned at the age of nine or ten. Do not dismiss such youthful dreams, because they often reflect solid goals.

But many more kids will have a hard time giving a single *real* reason. Here are some of the reasons that do **not** count:

- Everybody goes to college.
- My parents want me to go to college.
- I have no idea what else to do.
- Going to college will help me to figure out what I want to do.

For a venture costing an annual average of between $9,000 (state school) to $31,000 (private school), not including living expenses, those reasons no longer suffice. In times past, they may have had some merit. But for financial considerations alone, they no longer hold up. So put them under the microscope:

1. Everybody goes to college.
    a. Everybody does *not* go to college, although many teens think that.
    b. Some students have been given no other model to consider (military, vocational training, mission or volunteer work, gap years).

c. Potential employers in many fields are seeking skills not related to college attendance.

d. Any time a sentence starts with "everybody," be wary.

2. My parents want me to go to college.

a. Parents, is this something you have stated, or does the teen assume that to be the case?

b. Are you college-educated, and do you therefore expect your children to go to college?

c. If not college-educated, are you hoping your child will be the first in the family to get a degree?

3. I have no idea what else to do.

a. Are there ways to determine the best direction for a young person that won't take four years?

b. Could the development of goals be achieved through a means that does not cost thousands of dollars, often leaving a graduate with crippling debt?

c. Are there things of greater interest that attending college will not allow a teen to pursue?

4. Here are three more questions for teens to ask themselves:

a. What do the people you respect say about your readiness for college?

b. How do you plan to optimize every day of attending college, so as to justify the

c. What is your back-up plan if college turns out not to be for you?

As a life-long educator, I am fascinated to watch a national debate emerging about the new realities of the American college system. Surprisingly, the uproar is not fueled by ethical concerns about the slackened level of curriculum and disturbing aspects of professors and grading (subjects described in subsequent chapters). Instead, the scrutiny focuses on the crippling effect of the oppressive debt that now entangles what would otherwise be a college graduate's unencumbered path to get a job, start saving, buy a house, etc.

Whatever the reasons, I am glad to see college attendance coming under scrutiny. The misdirecting of so many students into college as the "default decision" after high-school graduation is a particularly American problem. In much of the world, people live with a system of restricted and highly competitive higher education. A university degree comes at such a high premium that the idea of "experimenting" with it would be laughable. Furthermore, secondary education in many parts of the world is designed to help young people discover and distinguish their talents, perhaps directing them toward skilled trades and vocational training. Those societies do not view vocations as a step down from college or in any way demeaning. In fact, vocational training has many obvious advantages. We have lost that tradition here in the U.S. and recouping will not be easy.

But remember, teens usually are not thinking about such factors. So, parents, let me offer one more strategy for conducting the discussion. Ask your teen to try to envision his life beyond the college years. Taking this approach will largely bypass the sticky issue of his readiness for college.

- Describe to me how you see yourself at age 26 or 30 (remember, 30 sounds awfully old to teenagers)?
- Where do you want to live?
- What kind of work do you see yourself engaged in?
- What will you do with your free time?
- What kind of material things do you hope to have (e.g. a cool car, walls full of books, the newest technology, chances to travel, the best set of golf clubs)?

Then explore the other side of the issue:

- What do you not want to happen in your life?
- What kinds of things do you absolutely not want to do?

Again, young people may not necessarily know all of the answers yet, but parents can recast those same questions *via* a retrospective sweep of their own lives and paths. What would a parent choose to do, or undo, if reliving the past were possible? What visions turned out to be false? What opportunities were missed? Also, if the parent(s) or other adults participating in this discussion did go to college, what were the real rewards as opposed to the illusory hopes? If recalling all of this seems too far in the distant past, wait for me to jostle the adults' memories in the next pages!

Most of all, I encourage both parties to have this conversation . . . multiple times! View these conversations as an important and potentially helpful exercise. They may open the door to some much-needed honesty. At the very least, such discussions can be filed away as a backdrop for reference in those the first weeks of college as the freshman drama unfolds.

18 *Why Freshmen Fail*

CHAPTER 4

Too Much

Many first-year students fail because they are burnt out before they ever get to college. By "burnt out" I mean generally exhausted by the rigorous schedule of too much daily activity over the preceding three, four, maybe even six or seven, years of their lives.

Think about the schedules many modern-day high-school students follow. They get up as early as 4:45 or 5:00 a.m. in order to finish homework from the previous night. They need to be at swim practice or marching band by 6:45 or 7:00 a.m. at the latest. Students then face a long day of classes, often occupied with time-consuming, non-academic activities unavoidable in a bricks-and-mortar school (bus time, security lines, home room, assemblies). Then, after classes conclude around 3:00 p.m., students head off to debate team or soccer practice. Even with a short commute, they perhaps get home around 6 p.m. or later. They eat whatever they can find (maybe not a healthy meal if mom and dad work long hours out of the house). An organizational meeting for a mission trip may come next on the schedule. Or, students who drive must frequently ferry younger siblings to and from music lessons or basketball games. Many older students will go to a part-time job. By 8:30 or 9 p.m., they sit down to do homework, but distractions like social media and

YouTube edge in, and so the real homework does not get started until 10 p.m. or later.

Weekend schedules for many high schoolers vary but tend to offer little relief as a different kind of busyness takes over. Thus, teenagers conceivably stay on a crammed schedule, day in and day out, for years. In this area, homeschooled students have a distinct advantage: they can generally organize their academic work into efficient and relatively convenient blocks of time, plus space their extra-curricular activities in such a way that there is still the possibility of a decent night's sleep.

Sleep? Ah, sleep! Now, you probably also have read that teenagers need nearly as much sleep as toddlers, since they grow at an extraordinary rate. Young people who stay on an exhausting schedule throughout high school will be bone tired by graduation. And I mean *bone* tired, as in deeply physically and mentally exhausted and unable to embrace college academic work and activities with the kind of enthusiasm they would otherwise possess. I have seen it over and over.

It does not matter that they are young. They arrive tired at the very point in life when they need to become self-motivated. Nobody will be there to push them, yet they stay too tired to motivate themselves throughout the whole first semester.

But wait, you say. They *need* these frenzied activities for their college profiles in order to gain entrance into prestigious schools and compete for the best scholarships. I fully understand that argument and the importance of building an eye-catching profile. But what if this kind of a resumé is not the only thing that catches an admission committee's eye?

I served for years on the panel at Southern Methodist University (SMU) responsible for awarding a limited number of Hunt Scholarships that the Dallas philanthropist Ray Hunt provided to cover all costs for four years of schooling at SMU, including a semester abroad. These generous scholarships were an amazing gift for the students lucky enough to receive one, which led to fierce competition.

But it may surprise you that the length of a student's portfolio was not the only or even the primary factor for us in choosing the recipients of these dream scholarships. More often we leaned toward the clarity of vision expressed by the student or the strength of ideas in the formal essay submitted for the application. Strong ideas and persuasive visions do not come easily to an exhausted young person. These things need reflection and, if you will, a certain amount of day-dreaming—impossible to attain if the fly-wheel on a teen's daily schedule never stops turning.

Okay, but wait (one more time!). That tired, pushed, burnt-out student will still have the whole summer before college to rest up! Won't that take care of the problem?

The answer is: no. Think about the typical post-graduation summer. First, both the student and family often feel quite nervous about the upcoming major changes. Kids get scheduled to visit every relative within striking distance. They have to earn money toward college or go on that last mission trip with the youth group. They want to serve one last time as camp counselors. They decide to cram in some kind of online dual-credit or community college course. They try to spend every free minute with friends. All of these good (even great) activities cannot help a student rest up or relieve the "burn-out" that has built up over the years.

Trust me on this one: it is hard to give your best to your schoolwork when you are wearied of everything involving school. Along these lines, I will mention the advantages of a gap year in the final chapter of this book.

I urge you, students, to take whatever steps you can to arrive at college as rested physically, and as peaceful mentally, as you can. This may mean working fewer hours, cancelling glorious volunteer opportunities, offending an aunt, or curtailing an anticipated family outing. But the cost is worth it, because no matter how excited students are about coming to college, if they have given too much on a daily basis for too many years, they will be burnt out. A burnt-out student will find it excruciatingly difficult to summon the waves of enthusiasm and dedication necessary for a successful first semester at college.

CHAPTER 5

Alone in the Crowd

Parents, you have *loved* your children. They have been the focus of your lives. You have worked tirelessly to provide the best for each child. Everyone has been involved—the relatives, the neighbors, the church. But upon their graduation from high school, things change. The world will not view your teens as you do.

A college freshman no longer finds herself surrounded by praise. Every person has to face this transformation to some degree upon graduating from high school. Losing our "specialness" as we grow up is a reality—one not always easy for parents or children to accept. Adults can testify to the difficulties of this transition. Take a moment to remember your own life. Whether in college, the work force, or the military, a "child" must function now as one of *many* adults out there. And each of us must prove ourself capable of doing the job.

Not only is "specialness" lost, but identity as well! Do any of the adults reading this book remember feeling anonymous in those first weeks at college? Many freshmen will experience that situation. In the senior year of high school, people focused so much energy on them as they took SATs or ACTs, chose a school, negotiated the terms, packed the suitcases, and enjoyed the rah-rah orientation events that it is almost inevitable to feel let down when classes actually start. After many months of excitement, ordinary Monday mornings dawn with the mundane worries of making it to class on time, getting through the reading lists, and finding clean socks.

Plus, for the first few weeks, everyone is a stranger, particularly at a big school with hundreds, even thousands, of new people from very different walks of life. It can be intimidating, especially if those people seem "tuned in" and more capable. Maybe they are smarter? Maybe they had better math preparation? Maybe they speak two or three languages? Yikes!

The first inkling of this kind of insecurity dawns during an orientation assembly. Parents, if you think back, you may remember a version of this scenario. The incoming freshman sits somewhere in a packed auditorium. The leader of the session says, "Look left." Everyone looks. "Now, look right." A moment of puzzlement registers on the students' faces as they look to the right. "One of you three will not complete your freshman year."

Whenever I bring up this scenario during talks, many adults in the audience will nod saying, "Yes, I remember something like that." This exact situation happened to me at Ohio University. Did I fathom that I would be the person leaving? No. Despite my gnawing doubts about going to college, I presumed I would succeed.

Let's draw a couple of lessons. First of all, most kids do not hear much about their chances of failure. Perhaps not really one out of every three students will drop or fail out in the first year (after all, the administrator speaking to us in 1969 needed to make a dramatic point, and even so, I still did not get it!). Nonetheless, the percentage of attrition is high. Colleges and universities know it and factor it into their spreadsheets.

Beyond that, today's college-bound teens rarely witness failure no matter what kind of high school they attend. Everything in our present-day culture proclaims only success, up to and including the awarding of trophies in sports to players on both the winning and losing teams.

Nor are teens used to the fact that nobody will cry any tears over their failures—at least not within the academic institution. A world where failure looms as a real possibility does not match up with the nurturing world most teenagers have just left. It does not mesh with a culture where we issue "diplomas" to robe-clad kindergartners. No wonder students will shake their heads and wonder: "What happened to my comfortable world where adults make sure everybody feels successful, no matter what the level of accomplishment?"

Adults know that world changes forever after high school, whether the destination is college, the military, or the workplace. Thus, parents need to prepare their teenagers for what this "change" will look and feel like. For example, when Professor Macintosh surveys the first class session, he won't know (or really care) initially who was an A or C student back in high school or who will *become* an A or C student in the future. Those things will reveal themselves in time. The bottom line is: neither professors nor teaching assistants are going to look at an 18-year-old student and gaze lovingly, appreciating his or her capabilities—certainly not the way parents, relatives, and teachers did back home.

Let me add another point: names. (I will say more about this under the topic "The Who and What Strategies" in Chapter 14.) A student, no matter how distinguished, will start out as just one more in a succession of similar names over the years. Think how many Justin's, Jason's, and Jennifer's have appeared on a seasoned professor's class rolls. (A more unusual name like Maude or Egbert may get your child noticed, but not for anything that matters.)

Plus, to a teacher, it sometimes seems as if it has all been one long semester. In fact, occasionally someone in my profession will look up at a student walking past the office door and say, "How is your semester going?" only to hear back: "Uh, I graduated *two years* ago! I'm just back visiting." Now that is embarrassing. But I have made such a comment! In fact, upon reflection I did remember that student's graduation and posing afterwards for a picture with her. But unless a storm hit during the ceremony and electricity went out all over campus, any particular graduation fades into dozens of similar graduations. (Perhaps parents of a large family can relate to this in terms of a parallel situation when they look up at a son or daughter and say: "You're *nine* now? How did that happen?")

I'm writing a bit tongue-in-cheek, but the fact remains, all teenagers will experience a loss of "specialness" in the years after high school. They will be anonymous, at least for a while. Some teens may find this a great relief, actually! But whether they like or dislike their new status, they will need to develop new ways to measure their abilities and worth.

This anonymity may stay true until a student's junior or senior year, when the student will take advanced courses in a chosen discipline. Chances to partake of a professor's expertise at a higher level, to participate in scholarly discussions, or perhaps even to serve as a professor's research assistant, will abound. At that point, the student will no longer be just a "freshman" and will have something to contribute. He or she may, once again, be special.

28 *Why Freshmen Fail*

CHAPTER 6

Real Life

A basic fact to consider for teenagers headed to college: they are not used to life being unfair. Sure, they complain about the "unfairness" they encounter either in high school or at home, but generally speaking, at this stage of their lives, they regularly benefit from a super-human effort to keep things fair, especially within the family.

Parents: how many times do you explain to your kids just how diligently you seek to operate "fairly" within the dynamics of your household? Do you sometimes even solicit ways to be fair to your children from your friends and colleagues?

The quest for "fairness" has taken over much of the discourse in today's social and educational culture. For example, various constituencies will scrutinize the "fairness" of activities within a secondary school rather carefully. A board of some sort oversees virtually everything that goes on in high schools (both public and private). Furthermore, parental dissatisfactions or concerns work their way pretty quickly up the ladder and may even receive a public hearing. No matter what kinds of unfair situations arise, teachers and administrators still have *some* accountability.

In shocking contrast, the world of higher education (academia) overflows with unfairness. Universities have multiple layers of operation that students rarely see and can barely imagine. Much of what drives the university machine today has little connection with teaching (particularly in big schools). Very few forces hold professors accountable for what they teach. When problems arise, the student will likely have available a formal grievance procedure and hierarchy of appeals, but new students cannot always figure out how to implement the process, or grasp the consequences of employing it (which can adversely affect their future studies at that college).

Beyond the larger issues, a dean or department head rarely looks at a professor's course syllabus or pokes her head into a lecture. No nicely packaged, pre-set curriculum dictates the material covered in most classes. No standardized testing affirms whether the course content has been properly presented or learned. Situations that would never escape censure in high schools (such as professors not showing up for class or using raucous language) occur regularly in the college world.

The umbrella principle governing American university teaching and research bears an admirable name: "academic freedom." Meaning different things in various parts of the world, the term nonetheless stems from modern history (no older than the 19th century, and primarily emanating from the early 20th). Whatever its noble origins, today it translates far too often into a kind of pedagogical chaos and lack of professorial accountability.

First-year students arrive at college expecting to have responsible adults in charge and reasonable rules to follow. Instead, they are likely to find themselves frustrated and overwhelmed, suddenly at the mercy of an unfair and uncaring system. Will the Academic Advisor walk over to the freshman dorm and say to a new student, "I am very sorry. It really is unfair that you couldn't enroll in one single class you wanted for your first semester of college"? Will a professor gaze out at a class of 120 students and say, "You know, I've piled too many titles on this Reading List; it's far too difficult, so let me reduce it by a third"? Of course not!

Parents, think back to your own experience. If you went to college or vocational school, was everything handled fairly in all of your classes? Can you recall any academic situations that seemed incredibly unfair to you? For example, would a professor likely acknowledge the error of including material from chapter twelve on a test that was supposed to cover chapters ten and eleven? Did someone say you had not turned in a paper, despite the fact that you knew you had submitted it?

Tales about just such "unfair" situations circulate within any group of adults reminiscing about their college experiences. Some ended well, but many had serious academic or financial consequences. Again, with the current extremely high college costs, enormous repercussions can result if something goes wrong with credits or majors.

But is this "unfairness" unique to college? Think about the workplace. Perhaps a supervisor said, "By the way, Miriam is going to be out for a month. We thought about hiring someone, but you are so good at covering her desk, we just want you to take it over." (This compliment is likely to be accompanied with a big smile, rather than anything positive for your paycheck.) Surely that is not fair.

Or, has your boss ever told you that a major project was due at a certain date and, then, someone from the district office moved the date up, sending everyone scrambling? When the quality of the project suffers as a result, hard-working employees will likely take the blame. Surely that is not fair either.

For that matter, we find some pretty interesting examples of "unfair" in the Bible. This is one of my favorite stories (Matthew 20:10-12), ringing as true today as it did centuries ago:

> *The workers who were hired about five in the afternoon came and each received a denarius. So when those came who were hired first, they expected to receive more. But each one of them*

also received a denarius.

When they received it, they began to grumble against the landowner. "These who were hired last worked only one hour," they said, "and you have made them equal to us who have borne the burden of the work and the heat of the day."

"They began to grumble" . . . because it absolutely was not fair. After all, some of these people had worked hard all day in the hot sun, while others worked for only an hour. Unfair, unfair!

The parable of Prodigal Son presents another story fraught with unfairness (as perceived by the older brother). But here is the one that always gets to me! I can never fathom that Moses had to go all the way through the Exodus, spending forty years dealing with those whiny people, and yet he never got to enter into the Promised Land. That just seems to me one of the most unfair stories I ever heard. But we can top even that one with the story of Job, right? Bottom line: these stories teach important lessons—lessons you might want to share and discuss with your kids before sending them off to college.

Parents, I am issuing an order to you here: you must tell your teens about the realities of the adult world, including the proliferation of unfair situations in almost any institution you can name. If you don't have your own examples to pull from—meaning you never had anything unfair happen to you in school or at work, then hallelujah! You are very fortunate, but please ask someone else to step in and lead the conversation because your child needs to hear this.

Meanwhile, at home, I encourage you to do the following: Point out the specific ways in which you strive to be fair with your children. Explain that this extra-degree of consideration will cease in college. Point out, too, that you strive to be consistent and reliable, and so do most of the people they deal with. Their high-school teachers will not likely tell them: "You know, I told you you'd have until next Tuesday to turn your rough drafts in, but actually, I want to take them to read on the plane this weekend while flying to my professional conference, so please have them to me by 5 p.m. tomorrow." But a professor might say exactly that.

Or, as a parent, you probably won't say to one sibling: "I realize it's supposed to be Jenny's week to do the laundry, but you know what? You did such a great job, you can just do it this week too." Yet a parallel situation may well occur in college when a student working on a group project has to pick up a fellow-student's load or see the whole project downgraded.

Talk with them about these things. One way or another, they need to get used to the bumps of life as they happen (and they will happen). Often in life, they will do the work and another person will get the credit. Or they will set a situation up perfectly, and someone else, benignly or not so benignly, will move the pieces on the chessboard when they are not looking, leaving *them* to explain what went wrong. And most of the time, they can do nothing about these unfair, stressful situations.

If you find yourself short on examples to share with your teens, let me leave you with one scenario that represents (to me) a particularly egregious type of unfairness that college students may encounter. I have heard dozens of similar stories from students seeking solace in my office.

A student's brother is getting married in late October of her first semester. After receiving the syllabus in the first class, she sees to her relief that the Friday she needs to miss for the festivities is scheduled as a regular lecture day. She writes a polite note to her professor, saying that she needs to fly home the Thursday night before that particular Friday to attend her brother's wedding rehearsal and the family dinner. So far, so good: she has done it the right way. The professor might even thank the student for thinking that far ahead and making the request the proper way. In addition, the syllabus lists the course's midterm exam date as one week before the day she will miss, so there appears to be no negative consequences to her missing that single class.

All *seems* well until a few days before the scheduled midterm, when the professor announces to the class, "I don't think we're quite ready for this midterm, so let's put it off a week and do it the following Friday." That Friday, of course, is the day of her brother's wedding rehearsal and dinner. She speaks to the professor later, saying she is happy to take the exam as originally scheduled, or on whatever day is easiest: she is absolutely prepared and ready. The professor, instead of commending her, says something such as, "I never give exams early." Or, "Well, then I'd have to make up two exams, one for you, and another for the rest of the class."

The student may be shocked by the not-so-subtle implication that she would take the test and then tell everyone else in her class its content. The realization dawns that she may have to make a choice between taking her midterm or missing her brother's wedding. About the time that realization hits her, the professor says, matter-of-factly, "You'll just have to choose which is more important: this wedding or your course work and degree."

What? Would a teacher really say something like this?

We, of course, hope that the professor's answer would be: "Oh my, your brother's wedding. Of course! I remember you gave me a note about that several weeks ago. So, let's work it out." That certainly would have been my answer, and the answer of many of my colleagues over the years. After all, the student had nothing to do with the schedule change. However, over the years I worked with some professors who would have no compassion in such situations. They would not see this clash as highly unfair to an organized and methodical student trying to do things properly! Instead, they would insist the student make the painful choice between taking a zero on the midterm (and getting on the plane as scheduled) or changing her travel plans even though it may result in missing the wedding entirely.

Is that fair? Absolutely not. Will something like this happen to your student in the first year of college? I dearly hope not. But at least prepare the incoming student for this possibility. Help your teen recognize that, alas, unfair situations come up throughout adult life, no matter how well we organize or approach things. And with that story in mind, let's tackle the biggest bugaboo about college: grading.

CHAPTER 7

The ABCs

Grading systems in college may puzzle incoming freshmen. The dynamics usually differ from those of the high-school years. Let me tell you the first fact.

Professors do not always grade fairly or accurately in college. Most parents know this truth, but incoming students may not realize it until far too many weeks have passed. That leads to the most important advice I can give to new college students about grading (not "study hard" or "turn your work in on time," although those are good admonitions). Are you ready?

Throw nothing away.

By "nothing," I mean *nothing* that relates to the classes you take. Not before the class, not during, and not even after you receive the final grade. Keep the course syllabus. Keep the bibliography and assignments. Keep even a one-page pop quiz on which you scored 100% (or 55%) and would otherwise crumple up and toss in the wastebasket. If all of your course work (including quizzes and tests) exists solely on the computer, print it out or at least save it to a cloud or external hard drive. Keep it, whether in file folders, shoeboxes or remote files—whatever allows you to preserve everything that has any bearing on the class.

Why? Because the wise college student keeps an accurate and well-documented record both of the requirements for the course and of his or her individual preparation, participation (attendance), assignments, and tests. Do this for *every* class. Unintentional mistakes can happen, and they do. Grading atrocities can occur, and they do. You can defend yourself only if you have your own documentation.

Parents, help students see these materials as "evidence," rather than pedagogical items. Explain how you handle the back-up documentation for your income taxes. Do you throw away your receipts and records? No, you keep them seven years. Tell your kids why. Students need to follow that same strategy until after graduation. Just because a class is over does not mean the danger is over.

Danger? Did I just use the word "danger"? How could I possibly talk about danger within a discussion of college grading? Parents who know the answer probably have already dropped their head into their hands, remembering their own experiences. For those who do not know, let me explain. First of all, the very fact that you even *took* a class and earned the credit can potentially disappear in the web of computer data that controls today's record-keeping. That may happen rarely, but it has happened—believe me! More importantly, grading can be, and far too often is, completely arbitrary in college. "Arbitrary" does not mean that individual professors have no standards for their classes. But those standards vary from well-honed and valid to utterly capricious. Having documentation of the work completed may be the only thing that saves you in a variety of situations.

Before we talk about those situations, let me expand on just how baffling and unpredictable college grading can be. For example, some professors will announce at the beginning of a class: "I give A's to no more than two percent of students in my classes, no matter what." Across the hall, another professor may say: "I expect *all* of you to get an A in this class *if* you do the work." In the middle are endless variations. Each new class requires the student to figure out how the professor grades. This might have been a pleasant challenge in years past, but, again, in an era where an individual course costs hundreds or thousands of dollars, the outcome of each class matters tremendously.

Most professors employ at least some automated grading: matching, multiple-choice or fill-in-the-blank, with a scanned answer sheet or on-screen boxes to click. This kind of testing is called "objective" (even though it can be subjective). The student immediately sees the score. In those cases, print out whatever you can, even though you have little room to argue with it.

A human being will grade tests with short prose answers, such as defining terms, or essay questions, as well as term papers. That human being should be the professor, although, all too often, a teaching assistant (T.A.) will be assigned to do the grading.

Some professors still personally grade every bit of a student's work, conscientiously wringing hands over Student A who always struggles, sitting back to enjoy the answers written by Student B (who nails every question), and applauding Student C who has improved greatly over the semester. A freshman with such a professor should rejoice.

But the polar opposite of that ideal situation prevails in far too many cases. Some professors never grade a single test or paper during an entire course; instead, one or more teaching assistants will bear that responsibility. The professor may not read the term papers or, at most, glance through them, again giving the job of "correcting" them to a graduate student instead. In many cases, the professor may not be the person to record the grades, but, rather, the teaching assistant.

Imagine this situation: the class has 180 undergraduates in it. The teaching assistant comes from a country at least 10 time zones away. At two o'clock in the morning during finals week, this poor teaching assistant has to record grades for Jake Mardel, Jake Martin, Jake Marvin, Jason Candor, Jason Cantor, Justin Truman, Justin Tumbell, Justin Turrell—all of these similar names listed on a little computer screen. Exhausted from a full semester of doing his or her own courses, exams, papers, plus an unreasonable amount of that professor's bidding, plus maybe even raising a family, very possibly this person will make a mistake wherein Jake Martin's final grade of 83 goes to Jake Marvin, while Jake Marvin's 63 goes to Jake Martin.

Now do you see why the freshman needs to learn to keep every paper? Without documentation, Jake Martin has little basis upon which argue the injustice of a grade two full letters lower than expected. (Jake Marvin will be dancing a jig, telling his friends that he turned out to be far more brilliant than anyone thought possible.)

While thinking about numbers like 83 and 63, let's consider another problem that an incoming freshman can find unfair, or at least disconcerting. In a large class, or if the professor chooses not to be engaged in the progress of the students, the grades will be issued based solely on a mathematical system. Forget the idea that Cody—who bombed the first test (51), met with the professor, then worked extremely hard to earn a solid B minus (81) on the second test, and nailed the final exam for a solid A (96)—deserves at least a somewhat higher grade than his 76 average would indicate.

Of course, not every professor would agree with that assessment. Some would say, "the grade is the grade, the numbers are the numbers," as well as, "plenty of students did *not* bomb the first test—so to them should go the higher grade." But to me (and to those colleagues whose grading policies I most respected), good teaching aims at assuring maximum progress and mastery of the subject, and that leaves room for interpreting the numerical results.

Someone might ask, "How did *you* grade, Professor Carol?" Well, back in those days, I slowly developed my own, and perhaps somewhat idiosyncratic, but consistent policy of grading. You would be surprised at my method, but I will say two things about it.

First, to me, college grading always seemed to be an art, not a science. I found it exceedingly difficult, almost mystifying, even after decades of wrestling with grading. The quality of preparation and effort expended by students in my classes varied enormously. The backgrounds of my students (primarily music majors) differed as much as their ages (from seventeen to fifty, or even older). A fresh-faced 18-year-old voice major from a farming town in Nebraska might sit in music-history class next to a 30-year-old veteran who, after years playing a trumpet overseas in the Army band, has now returned to school on the G.I. Bill to complete a bachelor's degree in music. Across from these two might sit a petite 18-year-old violinist from Seoul who began her serious musical training at age three. She has already played on a concert level for several years, knows music theory inside and out, and speaks three languages, the weakest of which, alas, is English. You tell me: how could the work of three such persons ever line up to be evaluated purely according to one numerical standard?

This mixture of students I just described is not unique to music. In virtually all college departments today, a version of this same multi-national environment and "spread" of ages and abilities characterizes many classes. Incoming freshman need to be prepared to find their place in the midst of such a mix.

The second point about my grading is something I am particularly grateful I can say. With few exceptions across the decades, students said that my grading was fair. A victim myself of some of the capriciousness of professorial grading, I never wanted students to identify me as such a teacher. Again, I saw grading as an art, and with any art things do not always follow the textbook. Nevertheless, I hoped to reflect the student's effort, progress, and product in each course grade.

Here's another issue. You may have heard rumors that the personal tastes or political views of the professor can play a role in the grade assigned. It's true. Far too many professors allow their own personal, political, or social agenda to enter the classroom. The student who will not agree, or at least play along, with this agenda (even if it means betraying religious convictions) faces direct consequences, some of which can influence the grading. (We will take up the topic of political correctness in more detail in Chapter 15.)

On a gentler level, some professors simply just have their beloved topics. Running jokes circulate among students to the effect that "to get an A," all a student has to do is write a paper about such-and-such (whatever that is) and, in it, say x-y-z. The professor will love it! How well a student flatters the professors' interests and position actually can influence grades. The unwritten rules of professional flattery may surprise teenagers, but adults should introduce the subject. On the other hand, a sincere admiration and interest in a professor's research interests will bring a student and teacher into a closer relationship.

All of these issues help illustrate my initial point that grading in college can puzzle or even bamboozle the incoming student. Part of the growing-up process involves being puzzled by situations, and then figuring them out, right? Certainly that is what these same teens did as toddlers, falling or banging their heads in the process. The comparison is apt in some ways.

However, I mentioned "danger" above. Let me close this chapter by recounting a particularly awful situation I witnessed involving an undergraduate. The student, a junior at the time, wrote and turned in a term paper for a fall course that represented quite a reach for him. He had to take this very difficult course for his major, and he struggled throughout. The professor had a just reputation for being brilliant, but enormously demanding and not accommodating. After taking and passing the exam, the student found an "incomplete" entered instead of a grade. The professor told him he had plagiarized in his paper. He was in shock: What? How? Yet the professor did not allow him to see the paper.

Not only did I know the student well enough to be certain he would not consciously plagiarize, but he showed me a printed out copy of an early draft of the paper (although not the final draft, which he had neglected to print out). What the student showed me in the draft did not lean toward a case of plagiarism. I did see a few places where an extra footnote might have staved off the problem, giving any professor a *perfect* opportunity to teach. Worst case scenario, the professor could have asked the student to redo the paper or write a different paper, and pointed him to material to help him improve his ability to document his work.

Instead, as spring classes began (when the storm should have passed), the professor decided to take the student to Honor Court. The rules for Honor Court clearly stated that violations must be charged in a timely manner, at the latest during the closing days of grading during the relevant semester. However, the Honor Court representatives ignored that important rule. Things escalated. Family and deans got involved, but nothing changed. The student was charged with plagiarism, convicted, got an F on the course and a mark in his record. Also, he had to pay over a thousand dollars to retake the course. Retaking it threw off his scheduling for the following semesters. It was outrageous, but no internal mechanism restrained this professor's actions.

Perhaps this student should have obtained an attorney and fought the charges. But, the family assumed that the Honor Court would act fairly (it did not), and they also were reluctant to incur hundreds or thousands of dollars in legal costs.

Recalling this situation, as well as similar ones I unfortunately witnessed during my career, infuriates me. But such situations happen in colleges. And students who do not take the steps outlined in this chapter will be helpless to defend themselves. What family considers this kind of ugly situation amidst the excitement of sending a child off to college?

So parents and students, be wiser than foxes, and recognize that it is up to *the student* to establish habits that afford the maximum protection from costly "irregularities" in the grading process.

CHAPTER 8

"Free" Time

A college class schedule looks deceptively liberating. Students may be thrilled by the liberating aspects, but precisely these can ensnare them. This particular pitfall hits me personally because it led to my first failure in college.

Depending on a student's background, a typical college class schedule seems "wide-open" with large blocks of free time. At the very least, it appears significantly less crowded than the one that regulated daily life during the high-school years.

A first-semester college schedule of sixteen credit hours might look something like this:

	Mon	Tue	Wed	Thu	Fri
8:00					
9:00	Eng. 101		Eng. 101		Eng. 101
10:00	Calculus I		Calculus I		Calculus I
11:00		French II		French II	
12:00					
1:00		Poli Sci 101			
2:00					
3:00			History		
4:00			Seminar		
5:00			"		
6:00		Swimming			

It looks rather empty, doesn't it? Just two classes on Monday-Wednesday-Friday; two on Tuesday-Thursday; a single history seminar (3 hours) on Wednesday afternoon; and swimming one early evening per week. Precisely this deceptive emptiness can deliver an inaccurate message that there is plenty of T-I-M-E in college.

Indeed, that false belief derailed my chances for success when I entered college. Suddenly I had oodles of free time (I thought), which gave me a green light to pursue whatever I felt like doing at the moment. I was no longer under momma's and daddy's roof, so I could just go here and there, visit with this or that person, and, oh, how I loved it . . . at least for a while.

That brings us to two hidden facts about the deceptive openness of a college class schedule. First, the issue of deadlines. When a freshman gets this type of class schedule, the important deadlines (like the mid-term and final paper) stretch into the future, many weeks, even months away. How marvelous it all seems to an 18-year-old, especially coming from a life where nearly every day in high school involved a treadmill of activities. Ecstatic freedom awaits!

Except it isn't freedom. A freshman can barely grasp how much preparation a serious college course requires. The class lecture may last only fifty or eighty minutes, but reading and assignments will demand three to five hours or more. In the field of music history, my students would need to dedicate four or more hours to careful listening of repertoire and viewing of video operas, ballets, or documentary films in order to be prepared for a single class. They also needed to do some reading. An upcoming test would require study time on top of that.

In addition, college classes demand multiple layers of preparation. A certain amount of social interaction connected to the classes will arise, such as study groups and group projects. Then the tantalizing array of events on campus (some connected to a student's academic interest) rush in and fill up significant time. Everyone needs time for basic tasks, many of which mom or dad possibly did in the past: laundry, shopping, cleaning, auto maintenance, etc. A student must schedule all of this carefully, or else that open-looking schedule will become a blueprint for disaster.

The other pitfall that affected me had to do with my mistaken sense of how much time stretched between class sessions. I would leave after a Thursday mid-day class, enthusiastically thinking: "Well, that's over. Great! Now I have six whole days until that class rolls around again (the following Tuesday)." Can you guess how I counted? The answer is foolishly! I counted Thursday (well, the day wasn't over yet), Friday, then Saturday and Sunday (a whole weekend!), Monday, Tuesday: six days. I know, I know, but that is how it looked to me as a 17-year-old.

So, here is my advice. Parents, have your college-bound kids practice saying this phrase.

There are NOT SIX days between Thursday and Tuesday.

Say it with them. Have them write it 100 times. Internalize it . . . whatever it takes.

To get them to look realistically at the preparation necessary for the next (Tuesday's) class, they need to absorb this sentence:

There are NO FREE days between Thursday and Tuesday.

That's right. None! To ensure success, the student must start thinking about Tuesday's class almost immediately after Thursday's class ends. For certain, there is "zero" time between the Tuesday and Thursday classes, or the Monday-Wednesday-Friday classes.

The problem of losing grip on the schedule can easily worsen with a single, once-a-week seminar, such as the one shown in the earlier schedule. That "full week" in between seems to stretch lazily into the distance. Watch out, because it will snare a freshman quicker than a mousetrap.

So, what is the solution? Actually, my recommendations are straightforward. Students: make a pledge to yourself that, if at all possible, you will devote approximately ten minutes after every class reviewing what happened in the lecture, the notes you took, and the assignment(s) for the next class. Those few, seemingly insignificant minutes will accomplish three important things. First, this modest process counters the temptation young people (all of us, really) have to fling a hard task off to the side, preferring to think instead about things more pleasant. Second, the brief time spent allows the student to remember (as in, not to forget) and to prioritize what he or she will need to do, whether by highlighting a reading list in a handout, writing explanatory notes to oneself in the margins, or making a list of tasks somewhere.

Third, a few minutes spent reflecting on the class that has just ended imprints on the young mind the ongoing responsibilities throughout the whole semester of any class in college. These responsibilities do not end when the day's class session ends. Attending the lecture is the opening step, nothing more. The real work (steps two, three, four) begins after the lecture ends.

In fact, learning to do this may result in a valuable life lesson for students. Parents, do you ever, after an intense meeting, sit back in your car and think through what just happened? Have you ever taken a few minutes after an event to review materials and consider what needs to be done? If so, you know the importance of time spent clarifying tasks: you can order them in your mind and put the critical items in the forefront. This operational strategy helps adults, and it will help students.

But remember, it contradicts what students instinctively want to do, which is toss everything out of their minds the minute they get out the door. So work with them on this. Help them learn how to organize the multiple layers of study needed to survive a typical college schedule and flourish.

That leads us to the class itself, but students cannot flourish there until they consider who is in the front of the room: the professor!

CHAPTER 9

Who Is the Teacher?

Students fail to understand the role and the psychology of "the Professor."

A professor presents a new kind of personality for most incoming freshmen. A professor is not Miss Betty the librarian, Mr. Scott the piano teacher, Coach Rick, or Mom. A professor may be a mom, but not the freshman's mom. Furthermore, generally speaking, professors are not the easiest people to deal with.

I refer not only to academic strictness, but also to what I call "the psychology of the professor." In this chapter I will explain some of the reasons why freshmen often struggle to adapt to this new world of "professors."

I have already referred to the fact that professors may lack empathy or refuse to be flexible. I happened to be on the softer side—one of those types who kept an electric tea kettle and a tin of cookies in my office, partly because I liked tea and cookies, but also because I wanted to know my students as well as possible. Yet, I have to say that those of us who approached college teaching this way are *not* the majority (and, parents, you likely know that from your own experience). A few professors offer cookies, but a good many more convey that they have limited time for students and would prefer keeping any interactions to a bare minimum.

Now, your student will likely encounter great professors along with the difficult ones. When I look back over my many years of study (from Bachelor's to Ph.D.), I was absolutely blessed by extraordinary professors. One or two were utterly forgettable (not necessarily a bad thing), but most were exemplary. I had a grand total of two negative experiences.

But I saw many unpleasant things, and heard even more. Over years of teaching, I listened (with tea and cookies in hand) as students wept out stories that could make your hair stand on end. Even factoring in the dramatic tendencies of young people, these ranked as bad situations—circumstances to avoid if at all possible. In short, students need insight into such situations and the job of "being a professor." Four main issues affect students.

Empathy

First of all, students, PROFESSORS ARE NOT WARM AND FUZZY. Dr. Bern did not earn her position at University-of-Whatever by being warm and fuzzy. In fact, a professor labeled as accommodating to students may draw ire from departmental colleagues (who are definitely *not* warm and fuzzy).

Also, there really is a specific psychology of a professor, bound up with what I call "the professorial ego." Parents may be able to recount specific stories about just this subject. In fact, their children may hardly believe what their parents recall, or forecast, about situations a freshman might encounter. Can the student do anything about the strange ways professors may sometimes behave, seemingly with impunity? The answer is: rarely, unless the behavior is so egregious that it draws public attention, and no student wants to be in that position.

Intensifying the confusion about how to relate to professors is a fact we already discussed, namely that incoming freshmen must cope with feeling less special once they become a member of a new academic community. Here's a tip: do not confuse the professor's distance from his or her students with meanness. Over time, students will come to understand and easily distinguish between "mean" professors and ones who are, in my favorite description, "curmudgeons" (possibly very funny ones!), distracted, or highly gifted with sarcasm.

Students need to discern how to communicate with such professors. They must learn when and how to approach professors if they want a positive response (more on this in Chapter 12). A head start on those skills alone can help enormously. With that said, we will move on to another sensitive topic.

Money

To start with, professors all too often have modest salaries. If a professor holds what is called an "endowed chair" (where a high-profile donation funds the position) or teaches in status-rich fields such as law, medicine, or business, then that person may make decent money. But for professors in the Humanities, such as English, foreign languages, history, literature, philosophy, or the arts, the salaries can be embarrassingly low, especially with recent shifts that give an increasing share of the teaching load to very poorly paid adjunct faculty. I actually did not want my students to know my salary. I wanted them to keep an illusion about how well we were compensated. For most of my formal teaching career, I taught in an esteemed, fancy private university. The entire "aura" of the place breathed elegance. My students presumed my salary automatically reflected the tuition they paid and the luxuriousness they saw around them.

It did not. In very few schools does the fancy level set by opulent buildings, professional stadiums, and glitzy dorms trickle down to the individual teacher. In fact, my salary actually *suffered* because I taught at such a private school. Professors in many state universities who shared my exact rank and experience fared better with their salaries, set by state legislators and matters of public record.

Parents, you know that being locked into a profession (no matter how beloved) with low wages is debilitating. Yet, that professor standing before the class studied through a bachelor's and master's degree, labored through a doctorate, then tackled brutal competition to gain a job, and may also have survived a rough process I will explain below called *tenure*. To do all of that and still have limited earning power causes great frustration. Trust me.

Tenure, Mobility, and Department Politics

Politics are awful in a university department. Yes, they can be awful at any job, even in a church or synagogue. But politics are really nasty for those who teach at colleges. The reasons for this nastiness impact the way professors approach their jobs and their students.

The two main explanations for professorial frustration are *tenure* and professional jealousy. Let's take on the "T" word first. Tenure comes from the Latin verb *tenere* (to hold): compare the word *tenacious*, which means strongly to *hold* on to something. Tenure in the college system literally means a professor gets to keep his or her job (as opposed to losing it). Students may not even be aware of the tenure system, and do not likely understand it, nor does the general public. It sounds very nice on the surface, but that surface has cracks.

Let me illustrate. A young professor, against all odds, gets a full-time job (as opposed to poorly paid, highly demanding part-time, or adjunct, teaching). The professor competed with 50, 100, maybe 200 or more equally (if not more) qualified candidates for the job. But fortune has smiled, and Professor Garrett has the job!

Fortunately, he found an opening in the right field, applied in time, had the application actually looked at (rather than shelved in a box, since the position was going to someone internal anyway, but had to be advertised). Professor Garrett survived the search mechanism, got an interview, and was hired. And while actually *getting* hired feels great, each professor knows the odds, and knows that the tenure system will make keeping the job difficult.

Thus, Professor Garrett works very hard. Basically, he works like mad for six years, publishing books and articles that, in many cases, no one will read, and writing grant proposals just to prove he can obtain them. And if Professor Garrett is fortunate, and the chairman and the dean smile, and the university-at-large responds positively, and . . . wait . . . oh, the students? Well, teaching will play a minimal role in the tenure equation, unless something goes very wrong.

To continue: if everything goes right, and Garrett's prayers are answered (and his *mother's* prayers are answered), and all paperwork is in order, and all sorts of other things go right that no one ever sees, then Professor Garrett may actually "get tenure," all of which means that he gets to keep the job. He gets a promotion to Associate Professor and perhaps a modest raise. If tenure is not granted, the college will give him a year to find another job, because Professor Garrett will be terminated.

That's right: if you don't get tenure, you're gone. Professor Garrett will need to find a job as a professor somewhere else. People across the workaday world experience that all the time, right? Yes, except most fields have something called job mobility. Even if fired, a good employee can find somewhere else to work in most professions (such as nurse, accountant, public school teacher, etc.). Nothing could be further from the petrified status of university teaching. Professors face a crippling lack of job mobility and systemic strictures that box in their careers.

It would seem that getting tenure solves the problem, but quite the contrary. Returning to Professor Garrett, suppose he *does* get tenure. After six years of intense labor, he opens that golden letter of congratulations that says he now has tenure. He can keep his job and teach until he's 75 if he wishes (at least in some schools). Maybe even longer.

But remember the issue of job mobility. What happens if he has landed this first job in a college in Montana, but he is actually from South Carolina and wants to live and raise his family there? Perhaps his research interests have to do with Colonial history. Perhaps he has aging parents in Charleston. Maybe he and his wife cannot deal with the Montana winters. Can he find an equivalent job in South Carolina? Very, very difficult. And if he does, it will very likely be without tenure, so he will have to start the tenure process *all over again.* So he stays where he is, which is what tenured professors generally do over the course of their long careers.

In most jobs, even in public school teaching (which has a tenure system), people come and go. New folks move in, people transfer, departments expand (or contract), and people retire. In short, a changing flow of talent and personalities keeps the dynamics of a department or company from becoming too stagnant.

In a college, if you go back and visit your department after ten years, you are likely to find four or five of the same six professors who taught you. They have attended more graduations and supervised more theses, but otherwise, not much has changed—except that they have become rather tired of each other. And when people are tired of each other (and of the particularities of that job), they tend to become critical, petty, unresponsive, or irresponsible.

Parents, do your best to explain a bit of this to your teens. At their age, they haven't had any reason to think about such things. Share with them how professional stagnation frustrates people or makes them a bit weird (because it does). Knowing this may even help them make better decisions about their own future career.

Regarding the second reason mentioned, professional jealousy, students need to realize that a peculiar type of jealousy between professors often takes seed and grows. Even though professional jealousy is found in every profession, this jealousy in academia can become intense and ugly.

Such jealousy-based relationships get started for a wide variety of reasons. In some cases, departmental funds are excruciatingly limited. For example, only one professor repeatedly gets support to travel to professional meetings, whereas the others pay out of their own pockets. Maybe one professor inevitably draws an enviously light teaching load, while the other three in the department have overloads without compensation. Injuries, real or imagined, fester across decades. Too little changes in terms of administration or departmental personnel to help flush these injuries out.

The snare of this jealousy can catch unsuspecting students unawares. Despite professors' high level of education and accomplishment, academia is one of the least charitable environments I have ever experienced. In fact, not uncommonly, two professors who share the same field and occupy similar positions (two history teachers, two German teachers, two violin professors) engage in a truly dark drama of jealousy and ill will. Such things should not occur, but they happen more frequently than outsiders can imagine.

Thus, students, tread lightly. Do not assume that the relationships between your teachers are kindly, or that they will be supportive either of one another or of each other's students. Be careful whom and what you praise. (I know this seems paranoid, but a bit of paranoia can save you.) In short, until you *know* the dynamics between your faculty members, keep your head down, open your ears, and do your work.

Now if that sounds harsh in any way, remember that I am writing this book to issue worst-case warnings that may help incoming freshmen (and all students) avoid stepping into the middle of problems—problems that stem from dynamics they never encountered before going to college.

Accountability

Lastly, in a nutshell, professors function with very little accountability. They definitely do not fall under the kinds of scrutiny common for teachers in elementary or secondary schools. For example, students in public, private, or home schools normally follow well-organized curricula. Class lectures and tests probably correspond to the textbooks and assigned material, and generally a departmental head of some kind oversees the individual teacher's lesson plans. If a capricious or madcap approach to teaching overtakes a classroom, someone higher up will find out about it and investigate.

Now shift to college—a world with almost no accountability, academically or pedagogically. The class title may say Botany II, but class lectures could end up being mostly about golf, because the professor really likes golf and follows it avidly.

Along other lines, some professors frequently miss class. Even more commonly professors will miss attending their own office hours. (More on how to handle that in Chapter 13.) Professorial behavior receives minimal to no scrutiny, which accounts for everything from not attending office hours to appearing in class unkempt to routinely spouting foul language.

Teens are used to high-school classes that more or less convey a logical progression of content. In college, they need to be prepared for what I affectionately call "the professorial straight line," which looks like this:

Could a professor's lecture really progress like this? Yes! Nearly everyone who went to college has had a professor whose lecture wandered from topic to topic, incorporating material that appeared to have little or nothing to do with the subject. Some adults remember classes where they never once understood what a professor was talking about in a whole lecture, or where they gathered with other students after class to compare notes and see if anyone understood the information. This can cause a student to feel caught up in a nightmare, especially in courses that require precision.

Still, in defense of the professorial straight line, a sophisticated discussion of certain subjects, such as literature, history, or the arts, does require the interweaving of topics. The narrative line of many of my lectures surely struck some new students as though they were negotiating a highway filled with roadblocks. On the plus side, the very squiggles shooting off of a convoluted professorial narrative could be the topic that catches a student's imagination. That person may decide to explore deeper, and end up writing a term paper or master's thesis about the very information that "didn't belong" in the lecture.

On a personal note, my own doctoral dissertation came from a side topic that burst out from such a convoluted "professorial straight line." That incident led me to focus on obtaining a microfilm of a manuscript from the Leningrad Library. That microfilm became the center of my dissertation and led to a U.S. State Department grant to conduct my doctoral research in the former Soviet Union.

From difficult personalities to pedagogical confusions to irresponsible behavior—professors present a new type of teacher to most freshmen. The wise student will try to understand, foresee, and avoid the professorial pitfalls that can derail the first year of college.

But in the next chapter, I will tell you the simplest, and yet biggest reason that freshman fail. Are you ready?

CHAPTER 10

Where Do I Need To Be Right Now?

Throughout the previous chapters of this book, we have covered seven reasons that cause college freshman to fail. Now, we will consider the eighth and most common reason students do not make it past their first year. This is the simplest of all, and the most easily avoidable, yet it causes enormous problems for students, in particular incoming freshmen.

Freshmen fail in college because they neglect to . . .

[Drum Roll, please!]

Show up.

That's it: show up to class! Failing to attend class causes more problems than new students can imagine. It stands out as the number one reason grades slip. It can lead to a student being dropped from a course. Not only did I witness this with countless students across decades of teaching, but I also experienced it in my own college years.

Yes, I "forgot" to show up. Skipping classes proved to be the pitfall that triggered my not quite ignominious, but certainly embarrassing, second departure from college.

So how does this happen? I knew when my classes took place, right? Still, sometimes a student really *does* forget to show up. ("Wait, it's Thursday? Oh no, I thought it was Wednesday. Yikes, what happened to

Wednesday?" Followed by, "Oh no, I just missed my 9:00 Thursday class...")

But more often than not, a student makes a lazy, foolish, or ill-informed decision to skip class. Laziness sometimes masquerades as "tired" (what time did that freshman get to bed last night?). Foolish means thinking that an absence here or there will not matter. Many students say that skipping classes is no big deal, but they are terribly misinformed. Yes, a legendary course does exist where students rarely show up and the professor does not care. But let me guard you against taking that standard as a guide to class attendance! So, freshmen, if you hear your fellow students saying "class attendance does not matter in Professor Arnold's courses," or "everybody skips," shall I remind you, that peers (a.k.a. "everybody") are not always renowned for steering you in the right direction?

With all the excitement of getting ready for college, parents (and teens) may have assumed that class attendance will not be an issue. The student never skipped class in high school, so why would attendance become an issue in college? No one may have ever mentioned it around the dinner table during those "let's talk about college" meals. Many parents confidently assert, "*Of course* my child will go to class."

Wait a minute, parents. If you went to college or vocational school, did you ever skip a class, or two classes? Even more extreme, did you ever get in trouble with a course because of skipping too many classes? Taking it further, did you (or anybody you knew) get *dropped* from a course by the teacher because of an excessive number of missed classes? Honestly think back and share your experiences with your teenagers.

Especially if the last situation occurred—one day you found yourself dropped due to skipping class—you must share this story with your teens. Surely it shocked you. How could that happen to you, especially when you had a "B+" average after the midterm? How are you going to tell mom? What will granddaddy think? And what happens if you now are below the minimum credit hours to keep your scholarship?

All of this fallout from missing *one* class? No, but missing one class opens the door to missing many classes. Let me tell you how it happens, even to people who have *no* intention of skipping multiple classes.

Take this situation. Late in one week, you are flying to your sister's wedding (another wedding, but this time it will not conflict with any tests, so everything seems fine). You have taken all of the proper steps, the professor has tacitly agreed it will be okay, and so, you miss a Friday class, but just one.

When you get back, uh-oh, you wake up with the flu early Monday morning, and a high fever, so you have to miss Monday's class. Fortunately you only have a gym class on Tuesdays, which you have never skipped. But then, yikes, you are still sick on Wednesday. So you stay in bed. Then comes Thursday's classes. Well, you are so lucky because you get an email saying the three-hour afternoon history seminar on Thursday is cancelled this week. Another day to stay home and get well! You feel great on Friday morning, but you go to your car to find a dead battery. Oops.

Now you are about to miss your fourth class in a row. Perhaps you can walk to class, but you get there, only to find a quiz for which you are unprepared. So you fail it. Or, you really cannot get to class. Yet the professor clearly stated in the syllabus that more than three absences will result in being dropped from the course. You now have four absences, so the computer system clicks into action, and removes you from the roll. It happens.

Do you see *how* it happened, though? Creeping quietly, a harmless attendance decision backfired and snowballed until it dictated the student's fate not only with one course, but perhaps with the whole freshman year. Parents, your students must understand this.

Moving beyond the academic issues of skipping class, students need to know another convincing point: the bottom line, "dollars and cents" reality. Let's take a typical 3-credit course in a 15-week semester with twice-a-week classes (Tuesday-Thursday). If this course costs $454 a credit (you wish it were that price) the total cost to somebody (parent, student, scholarship fund, or loan) is $1362. So, with 15 weeks, two classes per week, do the division: someone pays $45.40 for every class, whether attended or not.

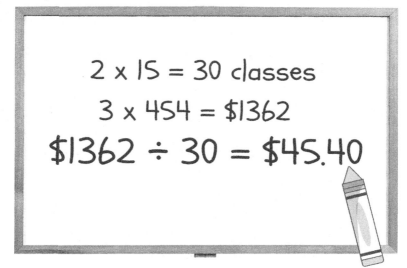

"Mom, those lectures aren't worth 45 *cents*!" your son or daughter might exclaim. Perhaps so, but it doesn't matter. Somebody, somewhere, is paying $45.40 for the student to attend each class session. Tell your student: "If a person walked up and offered you $45 dollars to sit in a climate-controlled room, prop your head up on your hand, and keep your eyes open for 80 minutes, would you take that job?"

As they contemplate that offer, remind them that they would never toss $45.40 on the curb, walk off, and leave it (which is what they do each time they skip a class). Also, remind them that it is far easier to sit bored for an eighty-minute lecture than to mow extra lawns in August or flip hamburgers every weekend in order to pay for retaking the class.

In short, it is a complete and absolute train wreck to miss classes: one car goes off the track and the whole thing smashes apart. A train wreck is a good analogy, really. I know I am belaboring the point here, but I do it for a reason. Teens can rarely see where one flaw can lead the whole train off the track, but it does.

We have couched this discussion around the negative consequences of skipping class. But think about the flip side: the benefits of regular class attendance. Most importantly, you will know what's going on. You likely will find that the lectures are the best place to encounter material that will appear on the final exam. You will know how the professor links disparate subjects and what points he or she emphasizes. You will likely find that your out-of-class preparation is far more efficient. The discipline you exercise by always being in class will likely spill over into all of your college activities.

I can vouch from experience and from the accounts of others that students who once struggled or failed in college because of missed classes find a completely different experience when they return to college with more maturity and discipline. They invariably realize how much easier college is when you stay on track. They get better grades, suffer less stress, and develop a genuine interest in the subjects they study.

Parents, impress this on your teens. College is their new job. And just as you show up for a job (because people tend to get fired if they do not show up), you show up for class.

Job? I keep saying job. Let me tell you why, as I review our eight pitfalls and turn our thoughts to Part II of this book.

RECAP

Let's list the reasons we have discussed for why freshmen fail:
1. They don't want to be there.
2. They are burned out.
3. They have lost their "specialness."
4. They don't expect unfairness.
5. They don't understand or cannot defend themselves against the grading system.
6. They mistakenly think they have "Free Time."
7. They fail to understand the role of the professor.
8. They skip class.

As you read through the eight major reasons freshmen fail, are you surprised by my references to certain topics? Many of the things I advocated (show up, be well rested, understand your boss and act accordingly, schedule carefully) as well as the warnings issued (keep careful records) qualify as good, old-fashioned job skills—the kind that pay off in any situation in life.

Did you expect these kinds of suggestions when you began to read this book? If not, I hope you were surprised and will consider them as seriously as any academic–specific guidance you will receive.

Notice too how many times I asked parents to look back into their own college *and* job experiences and share things they found unfair, difficult to resolve, or potentially derailing to their goals. Sometimes we, as adults, forget just how many "landmines" we negotiate on a daily basis in our jobs, volunteer work, and "family politics." At some point we all get wiser about deciphering human dynamics. We all have to learn to be prudent and cautious when assessing the actions we need to take.

Teens, however, do not automatically posses these critical life skills. How could they? So now, headed to college, they need to develop them, and the faster, the better. In short, entering college with Advanced Placement credit in physics is commendable, but knowing how to approach tricky dynamics of the workplace will solve far more of the kinds of problems an incoming student is likely to face.

Part II of this book moves specifically into the day-to-day dynamics of college life. I will describe situations that befuddle new students. Several topics will refer back to the "Eight Reasons" freshman fail, particularly Number Seven (the psychology of the professor). Other sections will suggest strategies that can make life easier for the new student. Also throughout Part II, expect more references to job skills as our discussion moves deeper into the inner workings of the college experience.

PART II

Tips for Flourishing in College

This second part of the book covers a variety of topics designed to answer a freshman's main question: "What do I do in this new world of 'college'?" I will not address issues of dorm or social life; those belong in a different book. Instead, I focus on issues that arise in the classrooms and academic departments where students take their courses, the places where they experience either academic success or failure.

The first chapters present ideas about how a student behaves and functions in class. After that, you will find suggestions about approaching professors, concentrating particularly on ways students can get the most benefit from the relationship in and out of class. Then, I will reflect upon the complex ideological environment found on today's campuses. The final chapters emphasize the extraordinary opportunities college offers—if and when a young person approaches the experience with sufficient maturity. Let me start with a fun, but useful topic: the "Nod Factor."

CHAPTER 11

The Nod Factor

Ah, the "nod factor"—one of my favorite subjects to share with incoming freshmen! I refer here to the actual *nodding* of the head up and down, and not to "nodding off" (zzzzz) in class.

On second thought, though, let me address the not-infrequent phenomenon of "nodding-off" in class. Students are famous for falling asleep in class. Yes, adults, too, are susceptible to the same problem, especially if sitting in a confined or airless space. A boring meeting, a long stay in a waiting room—these provide ideal places for nodding off.

Still, college students doze off in class for what we might call "preventable reasons," primary among them staying up too late the night before. With parents no longer around, freshmen may take weeks or *months* (alas) to realize that mom was right: teens need proper sleep every night! Wise freshmen figure out this issue quickly and regulate their lives accordingly. Less wise students can falter for a long time, wondering what is wrong and why things are going so badly.

Now, back to the phenomenon I call affectionately *"The Nod Factor."* Just what is it? The Nod Factor refers to something we all do, but may not recognize as a powerful means of human communication. In many cultures around the world, a slight nodding of the head signals recognition, acknowledgement, acceptance, and agreement. Theories vary as to why we, as human beings, nod, but whatever the reason, it is a natural human movement.

As toddlers, we learn to nod vigorously when we agree with something: "Yes, I want to go to the park," or "Yes, I want ice cream." We then learn to nod more subtly when we recognize information or accept instructions. As we grow, we begin to nod in even more sophisticated ways, such as indicating that we understand new content during the process of learning. By the time we approach adulthood, most of us have mastered a complete vocabulary of delightfully nuanced nods in virtually every context imaginable, some of them not necessarily happy ones.

Teens usually do not grasp how important and useful the vocabulary of nodding can be in their daily lives. Moreover, nodding instinctively *versus* employing the inherent power of nodding consciously—these are two different things.

So let's explore "nodding" by asking a question. Why would *nodding* be particularly important in a college classroom? I will offer you an example.

Let's say I am giving a lecture that outlines the development of French opera in the early 19th century. Dates and chronological associations will arise: for example, 1789 (French Revolution), 1793 (beginning of the Reign of Terror), and 1804 (coronation of Napoleon). When scanning the forty or so faces in the room, I look for my nodders as I initially present these dates. Why? Because these nodding students already know about this French history, at least to a certain extent.

In a class of approximately forty students, I would expect to see about five or six students who nod consistently as these points are presented. When I see such nods, I assume that these particular students: 1) have studied and *remember* the French Revolutionary period, probably from class work in high school; 2) recognize these dates as not merely numbers, but as indicators of events that engulfed every class of French citizenry; and 3) more or less get the point as to why I might bring these dates into a discussion of music history. Though perhaps I am too optimistic, that is my initial response to their nods.

Wherever the lecture material goes from that point, I know these five or six students will likely follow the topic right with me. Then, when I mention a specific point, such as the 1831 premier of Meyerbeer's landmark opera *Robert le Diable* where *en pointe* (toe) dancing first occurred on stage, I search for the one or two people who nod at that point. Those nodders usually will be a subset of my five or six. Often, these students will earn top grades at the end of the class.

Can I glean all of that from nodding? Yes, it's nearly that simple. Not guaranteed, of course, but likely.

In the meantime, I look for other types of nods throughout the lecture. Some students nod vigorously as they frantically write down the dates—possibly seeing them for the first time and recognizing the importance of this information based on my emphasis of it. Other students nod more slowly, working hard to make the historical and artistic connections. Either group of these nodders indicates, by nodding, that they are engaged both with me and with the material. They have an excellent chance of doing well in the course. They just need more time to catch up.

But then I see looks on other students' faces that are, well, let's just say the opposite of nods. Some stare off into space, wondering if any of it matters enough to write down. Others *nod off* (nap), text, crochet, fiddle with cough drops, or finish up homework for another class. They possibly have already learned everything I have to present that day and find the class very dull. However, my classes are not renowned for being boring.

The fate of these zoned-out students? Time will tell, but, for sure, they are not registered positively in my mind as "nodders." Of course, I do withhold my judgment about all students until I have concrete work from them in my hand (quizzes, tests, projects, papers), and I enjoy being proven wrong. Occasionally, a student who has seemed fully disconnected from *all* of the lectures ends up writing brilliant exams and papers, to my delight—but not often.

Looking beyond the issue of how the students will fare in the class, why should a student's nods matter to me, or to any professor? Because nods give very clear feedback to the person who observes them—in this case, the teacher. Whether or not professors seem to "care" about students, most want to lecture effectively. Much professorial griping about students has, at its root, long years of personal disappointment due to the inability to connect with, and successfully convey information to, a class of students.

Remember that your professors, even if jaded and crusty, are teaching material that has shaped their professional and personal lives, material they once cherished and pursued with passion. So even if they do not want to stand in front of that classroom on a given day, they still have a deep love in their hearts for what they teach. You might not see this love reflected in their faces, voices, or actions. But it is there, no matter how deeply concealed. Trust me on this one!

Students, maybe you are nodding right now, reading these last sentences. And perhaps you also are asking, "Does my nodding have to be sincere?"

Parents, step in and answer this. The answer is, "no." I am not asking students to be hypocritical or dishonest. I want them to understand that we often communicate non-verbally as adults, and some of it is artificially constructed to serve a greater purpose than may be apparent in the moment. So tell your teens about the many times in your adult lives when you have nodded, even if not so inclined. Think about the nod to one's boss that conveys: "Okay, I have no idea what you're asking me to do, but I will go find out and do it to the best of my ability." Or the nod that says, "That is so *not* a good idea (or it's one that is completely unfair), but until I figure out a better response, I'm nodding so we can get this conversation over with and I can get back to my desk and think it through."

So, I suggest that teens headed to college need to practice nodding, both observing nods analytically and practicing various nods for themselves. I really mean that: practice them. Do it in front of a mirror, please, so you can hone your technique. You might even want to take some selfie-videos, just to see how your technique is coming along. And students, start giving more attention to nods out in the real world. In any kind of group setting (an audience or congregation, for example), look around and see what kind of nodding you can observe. If you do this systematically, you quickly will see just how important, interesting, and encouraging nods can be.

One last thing. Don't let your nod become the grown-up equivalent of an obnoxious little kid shooting up a hand in class and yelling: "Call on me, call on me, I know the answer, I know the answer!" I also do not recommend that you nod like those bobble-head figures placed on shelves in restaurants or in the back of people's car windows. Like anything, nodding can be ruined by exaggerated use. Right? (Are you nodding? Good.)

CHAPTER 12

What NOT To Ask

Both in social situations and in the workplace, adults learn quickly what questions are deemed appropriate to ask. They learn which can be posed in public, which are best asked privately, and which should be withheld entirely. At least, adults *should* learn these things, since posing inappropriate questions in any arena can cause all kinds of problems. However, the idea of withholding a sincere question relevant to the classroom may surprise college students just beginning to cope with adult dynamics. But, believe me, learning what *not* to ask gives the freshman an edge.

So let me present two questions that a student should never ask. Understanding the reasons behind restricting these two questions can help a freshman evaluate the appropriateness of other questions that arise.

Number One: *Will this be on the test?*

Students, you do not want to ask this question. Definitely do not ask it in class or in any place where a professor stands in front of other students or colleagues. Depending on the professor, you may be able to pose a version of it successfully during office hours (see below). But if you do, you will want to reword it significantly.

Asking what will be on the test implies that the student's interest in the lecture material stems solely from a desire to pass a test. In other words, the student seems to be saying, "If it's on the test, I'll write it down and learn it. Otherwise, I don't care about it."

Generally speaking, a professor does not think about "the test" while lecturing. For example, when I lecture on a topic such as the role of the 19th-century novel in the development of Romantic opera, my head and heart are swimming with images and ideas I hope to convey to the students. I want them to be struck by the intense, cutting-edge subjects that 19th-century authors picked, and by the emotionally charged portrayal of the historical or legendary figures, as well as the drastic circumstances into which the authors placed these characters. Then, I want the students to draw connections between this literary content and the content of specific operas: plot, characterization, set design and costumes, as well as the musical grandeur. The *last* thing I think or care about is a "test" that will be given three weeks later. A student asking such a question at any point during the lecture will jolt me, and everybody else, fully away from the flow of my lecture.

Now even if thoroughly enamored of the lecture, the student *does* rightly care about the test coming up in three weeks. He or she will have to sift through vast amounts of material to find the elements most useful in preparing for that test. Naturally, this student wants to know and, you can argue, has the right to know. But the way to find out is *not* to ask that question, particularly any time during the lecture.

I call the second question to avoid the double-whammy, especially if a student has posed the first one repeatedly.

Number Two: *When will we get our papers back?*

Again a reasonable question, right? If you work in an office, you can reasonably ask: "When will the Divison Office send the figures for our quarterly reports?" But within academia, this particular question is a loaded one. First of all, the real answer may be "never," although professors rarely state this in writing or out loud. Wait a minute! *Never*? How can that be?

Sometimes professors give students an official reason, usually one explaining that the professor does not want future students to have access to test questions or completed term papers. The only way to guarantee this is not to put these items back in students' hands. In a best-case scenario, professors with this policy may invite the students to come review their papers during office hours, but they still will not release the papers to the student. The professor is not completely wrong in holding this kind of policy. Unfortunately, there often can be a kind of underground exchange of exams or term papers in some departments or schools. This dishonest activity may even involve the exchange of money.

But as a professor, I had a simple and clear solution: I always changed my test questions and term-paper topics. I even told students to feel free to consult old tests, if they felt it would help them to see the kinds of formats I used and types of questions I asked. I assure you, though, that my approach was more the exception than the rule because of the extra work involved. Many professors do not change either their syllabuses or their testing materials, even across many years of teaching. Since they give the same exams over and over, you can see why they might withhold returning them.

But other than guarding the material to keep the testing mechanisms secret, is there is another reason why professors would not give back papers? Yes. Are you ready for it?

The professor probably hasn't graded them. Not yet. And maybe not ever.

"What!?" you say. "How is it possible the professor hasn't graded them? We took the test four weeks ago!" Parents, if you attended college, you need to start explaining this odd phenomenon to your children, who may not believe it, even when you tell them stories from your own experience. For starters, relate all of the creative excuses given to you by your own professors. Perhaps one said, "Uh, students, I was busy preparing a research paper for a professional conference." (Maybe he was, but maybe he and his colleagues were playing golf.) Another professor might say, "Your papers are next in line after I finish a very time-consuming set of such-and-such papers." There may, or may not, be a such-and-such set of papers, but it doesn't matter.

I am not out to malign my profession. I know many professors who diligently grade each and every quiz, test, and page of the term papers. They give everything they have to help promote the educational progress of their individual students who usually will remember them kindly. But if you listen to people recounting college memories, you hear far too many stories about the professor who seemed not to care at all, who stalled on paper grading, or reneged on returning papers altogether. You will also hear countless stories about professors whose grading seemed capricious, incomplete, or disinterested.

In defense, I should add that grading papers is the least attractive part of a teacher's job, whether a person teaches 4th grade or doctoral seminars. Facing a stack of tests or papers either confirms a teacher's effectiveness or reinforces failures. Plus grading is tedious. It often requires correcting the same mistakes repeatedly. Occasionally, the professor does find papers that delight, surprise, and inspire. These are like chocolate bon-bons or a sparkling fountain. But the vast majority of one's grading time feels more like slogging uphill.

Yet, grading papers is, or should be, a big part of a professor's job. Perhaps students already realize that often grading is shuffled over to the teaching assistants: sometimes openly, in cases where marking papers is objective and could be done by anyone, but sometimes covertly, where the teaching assistant does all the grading but the professor claims the credit for the hard work.

Remember when I spoke in Part I about how professors work often with very little oversight? In any other business, a principal figure who did not complete a major part of his or her duties would face repercussions. But in academia, it is a rare dean or department head who intervenes in professorial behavior. Intervention does happen, but it takes quite a bit of evidence to make a case against a professor and follow it up. And the student who presents such a case may face unexpected repercussions of various kinds.

Nevertheless, if grading papers is supposed to be done, and papers are not being returned, why should a student not ask the key question, "When are we getting our papers back?" In short, this question casts a spotlight on the professor's inadequacies, at least in this capacity. Except for situations of illness or emergency, a professor ought to prevent the question from ever arising by routinely grading and returning tests or papers promptly. Yet, it can be a kiss of death for a student who brings up the matter to a professor, particularly in class, especially more than once.

So what do you do? If you realize, or hear from other students who have had this professor previously, that getting papers back is a problem, do the following: 1) make sure you make photo copies of your papers or any work submitted. This is *already* part of your plan to document everything you do anyway, right? 2) If you have heard, or suspect, that an inordinately long time will pass before you get a quiz or test back, then grab a piece of paper immediately after you leave the classroom and write down what you can remember about the questions to the degree you can. That way at least you have something to study by for final exams. Why is this particularly important? Many professors create final exams partly (or wholly) based on tests taken earlier in the semester. Plus, if you left the classroom thinking that the questions were fairly basic, easy even, yet a C- or D suddenly appears in your online grade book, your sketched-out notes will help you piece together a protest more authoritatively than if you've forgotten the details of the test.

Does this all sound drastic, paranoid, silly even? Perhaps it does. But remember the maxim: "Better safe than sorry." Experienced college students will tell you that you must be your own defender.

Now before I end this chapter, I promised a word about how to ask these two no-ask questions appropriately. There is a way, but first you must be in the right locale, preferably the professor's office. Other locales might work if you happen to bump into the professor at a coffee shop and he or she invites you to sit down and visit. However, in that case, you probably already have a professor who diligently returns papers!

At any rate, once in the professor's presence, you might frame these questions in the following manner:

> *Professor Salzedo, I'm trying to study ahead of the mid-term. In prioritizing the material, I wondered if the topic you covered today is one I should be emphasizing right now, or will you be . . . (get creative) following it up with more detail in next week's lectures?*

Or,

> *In my term paper, I realized that there were two possible solutions to the dilemma. I stressed the first solution as a better option, but I'm especially interested in seeing what you think of my approach. Will we be getting those papers back with your comments soon?*

You can find other ways to ask the questions, but either of these suggested approaches engages the professor in a discussion of the substantive material in the course—something he or she cares about—rather than merely the process of your getting it done and over with. Professors rightly view themselves as *teachers*. They are not simply administrators who hand out college credits for passing work. So approach the professor acknowledging this distinction.

Let me emphasize this. I really do believe that at the heart of every unresponsive professor lies a teacher who wants to share his or her passion for the subject. So your goal is (or ought to be) to learn the material well and make the connections. Demonstrate to the professor that this is your goal, and he will likely respond favorably.

If your only aim is to get a decent grade, then broaden and deepen your goals, particularly in preparation for those times when you have contact with the professor, which brings up our next topic for discussion.

CHAPTER 13

The Adventure of Office Hours

So far, I've made several references to something called "office hours." Outside of academia we use that term to indicate the times when a doctor's or dentist's office is open for patients. But in academia, "office hours" refers to those few (and they are few) hours a week when a professor is supposed to be sitting in his or her office, available to help students without a prior appointment. Notice, please, that I used the phrase "is supposed to be." Just because a system is designed to work a certain way does not mean that it will. Let's look more closely at this mysterious institution.

First, why do office hours exist? They are supposed to provide an opportunity for students to obtain one-on-one aid from their professors—a chance to go over problematic material, discuss challenging questions, and seek everything from suggestions for upcoming projects to references for future academic study.

How many office hours should a professor offer? Well, departments vary in their requirements, but five hours a week is about average. Now, five may not seem like enough for a professor to be available to dozens, even hundreds, of students. But the real issues with office hours involve not how many hours a professor lists, but rather 1) *when* the professor schedules the hours, and, 2) *whether* the professor actually meets or keeps the office hours.

The problem of "when" office hours are scheduled looms large because some professors fail to take the class schedule of their students into consideration. For most undergraduates, the mid-to-late morning hours, as well as early afternoons, are usually filled with classes. Thus, if a professor posts office hours as 10 to 11 a.m., on Monday, Wednesday, Friday, plus 1 to 2 p.m. Tuesday and Thursday, these hours, while convenient to the professor, will not be convenient, or even possible, for students who have classes during those times. Yet some professors, year after year, choose these prime hours because it means they can compress their required on-campus schedule and avoid extra trips to campus. Super-convenient scheduling for such professors trumps the desire to make themselves available to the students who need their help.

What would be ideal hours for students? Well, students tend to be more available in late afternoons, or very early mornings. I found the greatest results for office hours when I scheduled them at around 3 or 4 p.m. Now, to be fair, professors often will offer, "hours by appointment also." Students, when you see that provision, take the offer seriously. Call or email and ask for those appointment times that fit well within your schedule. If you don't ask, you will never receive!

Scheduling is not the only problem with office hours. Professors do not always show up for their office hours. Nearly anyone who attended college has either witnessed or directly experienced a professor not showing up for office hours. The reasons can be legitimate—an illness or emergency. But sometimes the reasons involve simply not coming, or arriving so late that a substantial part of the posted period has elapsed.

The Adventure of Office Hours

How can this be? Unlike in middle and high schools, students are not the professor's first priority. The college system does not revolve around the teaching of undergrads, despite what the brochures say. As described earlier in this book, an invisible layer of bureaucracy, research, and professional concerns drives most professors' daily schedules. Professors exceptionally devoted to mentoring their students have to squeeze in teaching and student concerns.

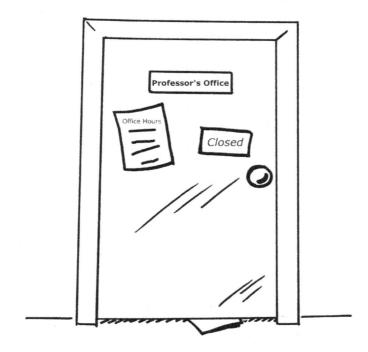

Office hours, then, may be the only "officially sanctioned" opportunity to cultivate deeper professor-student contact. Let me add, though, that in this new era of cyber-communications, office hours gradually are becoming an outdated provision. I personally regret this turn of events, but more and more professors are resorting to message boards, chat rooms, email and text communications, and even Skype and Messenger as primary vehicles of connection to their students. These technologies have a great deal to offer, and I can extol their virtues at length. But nothing replaces the traditional paradigm when a professor opened up his or her office and sat several times each week waiting solely for student visits and student inquiries. Fortunately, most schools still require professors to post office hours and hold them.

So now, having said all of this, let's return to considering what office hours are, and what they are not. Office hours present the best, and sometimes only, built-in opportunity to receive one-on-one, face-to-face learning from your professor. They can serve as a valuable chance to ask questions, overcome confusions, and extend your ideas to the professor. Ideally they turn into a dialogue. Less ideally, but more often, they become an individual tutoring session, which, if properly used, can improve a student's classroom performance and final grade.

So what are office hours *not* intended to be? Well, a visit full of complaints will not go over well unless the gripes legitimately refer to problems with class logistics (i.e., the book store has sold out of the textbooks, some of the required reserve articles are missing from the library, the T.A. has failed to show up for tutoring sessions). But griping about how hard you find the class, or how difficult the tests, will not win you a great deal of professorial affection and understanding.

What if the class lectures *are* too hard, or the tests too difficult or patently unfair? The student needs to be cleverer than a fox to find ways to get that point across in a positive manner. Consulting with upper classmen or a sympathetic counselor or administrator can help a student learn subtle ways to frame "complaints." The professor is not hired because of a talent for customer service, so you must remember, above all, to keep limited expectations and be extremely diplomatic when you do voice complaints.

However, there are more negative ways to use office hours than complaining. Let me give you an example. A student has missed several classes—perhaps with a valid medical excuse, and perhaps not. Either way, quizzes and tests have not gone well. Suddenly the semester is two-thirds or three-fourths over. Even worse (and far too typical), the student is staring at professor's door for the *first* time just days before the final exam.

Oh, those professorial offices do get busy the last week before finals! In fact, here is a good time to mention why many professors abhor office hours. They will sit for weeks, and almost no one comes by. Then, the situation becomes comical, as students who have never asked the first question in class, consulted a T.A. or tutor, or darkened the professor's office door, suddenly burst in and confess a burning interest in the course, and beg for the professor's mercy. So, students, my best advice to you would be to follow some version of the following three-step program.

Step One

Within the first two or three weeks of the class, drop by the professor's office during official office hours. If the professor is free (not with another student), stick your head in and introduce yourself, identifying specifically which class you are in (see the "Who and What" Strategy in the next chapter). Prepare in advance something at least slightly interesting or relevant to say.

For example, you may wish in advance to research the professor sufficiently to be able to make a comment about his or her background or publications. Get some help with this if necessary. Searching for information about someone before a meeting is standard practice in the business world. For example, you may be able to mention that your aunt also did her undergraduate work at UC Berkeley. (Not fascinating, but since the professor did a bachelor's degree there too, at least it is something.) Or perhaps one of your favorite high-school teachers served in the Peace Corps about the same time as this professor (who knows, maybe they knew each other). Or, you can say that you had hoped to take Advanced Physics in high school but there was only one section and it met at the same time as your third-year French class, so you are *very* glad finally to be doing it. Or maybe you hope to be able, once a junior, to join the study-abroad program which this professor leads.

Plan a short visit, five minutes or less. You professor may nod (remember nods?) in bemusement or boredom, or may respond quite warmly. It doesn't matter. You have done the responsible thing. Wear something nice when you go (that is, not your tackiest clothing), speak politely but not cloyingly, and then leave.

Step Two

It's a good idea to check back by mid-term, even if things are going well. You can simply pass by the door (if the professor is there and the door is open), and mention how surprised you were by such-and-such article on the reading list, or how you really struggled with Chapter 23 but the lecture yesterday cleared up many of your questions. Find something to say. The professor might simply tolerate you, but he or she might encourage you to come in and relate some of the points that had puzzled you in the chapter, so make sure your opening conversational line has some validity to it!

Step Three

Now this varies. If you are having trouble with the course, do not *dare wait* until the last week before the final. Get in there at the 60% mark again. Or the 70% mark. Ask for help. The key point is, you are not a stranger. You have visited before, and the professor will at least know who you are. He or she will be more inclined, almost always, to help (or at least set you up with some extra tutoring from the T.A. or the Learning Center). Even if you are not having trouble with the course, I suggest making a third visit two weeks before the end of the class. Again, it should be brief. Simply pop your head in and tell the professor how much you have enjoyed the class. Or how helpful, challenging, inspiring, or enlightening it has been.

What do these visits accomplish? Well, you'd be surprised. No matter what happens, you aren't an anonymous stranger. You have what we might call "a leg to stand on" when you appear tear-faced at the door after you've bombed the final. You also have cultivated a possible source for a job or scholarship recommendation if you do well in the course. At the very least, you have learned and practiced valuable people skills that will help you for the rest of your life.

CHAPTER 14

The "Who and What" Strategy

My good friend, a judge who also holds a doctorate in sociology, has a "talk" she gives to teenagers she counsels. She calls it the "You're Not Special Anymore" speech. It issues an abrupt wake-up call to young people and applies not just to those in trouble with the law, but to kids entering college, the military, or the work-a-day world. She addresses it particularly to those who have basked in the loving glow of parents, neighbors, teachers, and church family. (She has a different talk for teens who grew up in bad situations.) "Sorry," she begins calmly:

> but the time has come and you aren't going to be so special any more. The world expects you to stand on your own two feet. Furthermore, a new generation of cute, younger kids is coming right behind you, demanding (and deserving) the same attention you got from those who cared about you.

Depending on how she gives this speech (kindly or brusquely), her words can come as a shock. Yet, adults know it's true. They recall facing the transition from "kid-therefore-special" to being a regular person, faced with the daily problems that beset grown-up life.

The transition to adulthood often coincides with entering college. As we discussed in Part I, it can smack a student hard to confront a distressing sense of anonymity on campus. Especially if attending a big school, a new freshman sees no familiar faces. Instead, the student is surrounded by hundreds, even thousands, of strangers—none of whom particularly cares who he or she is.

Well, let me share the flip side of the coin. Every semester, professors are confronted with dozens, or hundreds, of new, unfamiliar faces. And while the professor is experiencing no particular trauma from this (as would the freshman), the situation for the professor can be difficult and has some parallels with the student's situation.

Therefore, in this chapter let me give students a simple piece of advice called the "Who and What" strategy. Implement this strategy immediately and consistently. If you do, life in college (and beyond) will be easier.

The "Who" Factor

The first part of the strategy involves the "Who" aspect. Freshmen need to learn to introduce themselves properly, not just the first time they meet professors, but repeatedly. Some teenagers have not been taught how to identify themselves in social or professional situations. After all, everyone knew them back home!

So, before coming to college, practice the following formula for identifying yourself to your professors—at least the first several times you approach them. You will need to state:
 1. Your name
 2. Specific course or lab in which you are enrolled
 3. One added quality

For example:
1. Hello, I'm Jessica Raddis.
2. I'm in your Tuesday-Thursday 11 o'clock British Literature class.

So far, so good. But what about this "added quality"? Here are some models:

1. I usually sit over by window. (added quality—helps professor visualize you in class)

or

2. I'm the one who asked your opinion about *Downton Abbey* last week. (added quality—particularly positive if the professor liked and discussed the question)

or

3. I'm the one who races in right at 11:00 . . . I'm so sorry, but I have to run from my 9:30 class in Morris Building. (added quality—shows your awareness of the need to *be* on time and your effort to get there, plus it helps cushion the situation if you're ever late)

Don't despair. You will not have to present all *three* pieces of information each time you approach the professor. You can quickly drop the "added quality" category, unless too many weeks have passed since you last spoke to the professor, who now has forgotten you.

Still, each time you initiate face-to-face (or email, text, telephone) contact, continue to offer your name and identify the course you're taking. Do this until the professor clearly has stated, "Oh, yes, I know you, Jessica."

Do not take it personally if it takes weeks for the professor to sort you out. Your face and voice blends with hundreds, even thousands, of previous students over the years. I cannot tell you just *how much* students of a certain age resemble one another, particularly young women with pleasant smiles, long hair pulled back in clips, and college sweatshirts!

It's almost unnerving. Sometimes, even when I fully know that the student standing in front of me is "this year's Caitlyn from my Opera History class," my mind sees a long line of girls who uncannily shadow Caitlyn's appearance. And several of them probably were named Caitlyn!

The same holds true for the male students, by the way. Undergrad boys tend to be fresh-faced (whether scruffy or clean-cut), clad in the same kind of jeans or khakis, wearing the same T-shirts and dragging around similar backpacks. For years, my roll was dominated by guys named Robert, David, and Matt. Then came the generation of Jasons, Justins, and Coles. Now rolls are filled with ambiguous gender names like Brook, Casey, and Reagan. Can you understand why a professor seems "absent-minded" when trying to sort all these people out?

But the bottom line is, kids at certain ages look strikingly alike, especially to a professor who has spent a lifetime teaching this age group. So while a class of 300 will be able to identify Professor Jordon immediately (that funny little bald guy with the baggy pants), Professor Jordon will not be able to sort out 300 new faces as quickly.

The "What" Factor

Now let us consider the "What" part of the strategy. In a nutshell, learn to use specific nouns when you ask a professor about something. Avoid pronouns. Do not ask a professor about "it" or "them." A college professor confronting these questions will not know what the student is talking about.

"Did you get it?" (a reworked draft of a paper sent by email)

"Did you fill it out?" (a reference form)

"Did you find them?" (test corrections slipped under the professor's office door)

"It" means nothing. Neither does "them." Plus, in a given week, especially as the semester progresses, our beleaguered Professor Jordon will be asked about hundreds of "its."

Why would this specificity be challenging to a freshman? Because for years, "it" and "them" are the pronouns a child has used to ask questions of a parent. Parents are tuned in the child's needs. Upon hearing "Momma, did you find it?" a mom knows exactly what the child is asking. A professor does not. So, here is the quick and easy solution. Use this formula:

Instead of:

> *"Professor Jordan, did you find it?"*

Ask:

> *"Professor Jordan, did you find the manila envelope with my biology project that I slipped under your door late last night?"*

Aha! Now Professor Jordon can say "yes!" because he nearly slipped on that manila envelope stepping into his office early that morning. Even if he has yet to open the envelope, he has a pretty good idea that he *got* it.

What are the benefits of learning to introduce ("Who") and specifically identify your request ("What")? First and foremost, it keeps the professor from feeling stupid. *Any* time you can save your professor (or any other social or professional contact) from feeling momentarily confused, awkward, or stupid, you are doing a good thing, both for that person and for yourself.

Secondly, a question stated clearly calls forth a better answer (certainly, a quicker answer). If the question is specific, the professor can move directly to something else, which might include offering helpful comments about the project outline rather than wrestle mentally to identify the amorphous "it."

Thirdly, the professor will carry away a sense of the student as a mature, serious person. And, like any other impression, this positive impression can be added on to other positive impressions, such as those garnered from the student's serious handling of office hours or good attendance record (the student has shown up to class, remember?).

Here is the bottom line: very few grades in college are strictly objective. Yes, some are, particularly if the computer is assigning the grade. But, in many cases, a professor wavers between assigning a B+ or A-, or even a C- or C (which can make the difference between losing or keeping a scholarship!). So *any* time you can show yourself to be serious, thoughtful, and "clued-in," you are storing up good will for the period when grades are entered into the record.

Most importantly, learning to present oneself clearly and to ask specific questions benefits a person throughout adult life. Helping the other person make the right connections puts that person at ease.

Try to imagine yourself sitting in a professional conference. Someone you vaguely recognize approaches and says, "Hi, I'm Walter Smith, the representative for the Southeast Region, and I believe we met last year at the planning session for the new accounting system." Kind Walter Smith has just saved you the frustrating process of trying to recall his face and reconstruct the connection. You will not need to fumble around for what to say. Your conversation has started on a positive note and can continue in fruitful ways.

Start practicing now, students. And if you catch your parents or siblings *not* being specific in their day-to-day questioning, you can gently coach them in this useful life skill.

CHAPTER 15

What Not To Say

The Betrayal of Freedom on Today's Campuses

Freedom of speech has long been a basic tenet of American life. Yet, freshmen entering American colleges today will walk across a minefield that has compromised or obliterated this freedom. Without an awareness of the ideological conformity that dominates campuses today, an incoming student can stumble into awkward, unpleasant, or dangerous situations. Does this sound serious? It is, so let me explain.

Political correctness, or P.C., refers to an ideological doctrine that has rapidly redefined our Western culture. It diminishes values long cherished throughout the West, particularly in the United States: freedom of association, freedom of religion, free speech, advancement by merit, and creative freedom. These values prevailed in previous generations and, until recently, could be taken for granted. But on today's campuses (and broadly across our society), such values are being replaced with a rigid, pre-determined roster of ideological viewpoints that faculty, administrators, and students must express (outwardly, at least) and follow in their daily actions. Failure to do so will earn punishment as simple as chastisement or as drastic as removal from campus.

106 *Why Freshmen Fail*

Because we in America have embraced the benefits of a college education, many people outside academia may find it difficult to acknowledge the deteriorated environment. Parents busy raising their families and making a living may not believe that campuses have become dangerous places for their children to express even a *single* idea contrary to the dogmas of political correctness. On the other hand, if you already have children in college, you may have heard stories that give you pause. Still, perhaps you reasoned that these troublesome accounts were isolated events. They are not.

How did institutions traditionally viewed as beacons of free expression become bastions of angry ideology, aimed at stifling individual freedom and replacing it with an artificially constructed system of unreal conclusions? It happened over time, and like far too many things in history that creep insidiously into place, this movement sneaked up on us. Some scholars place its origin at the beginning of the 20th century, in the years of social revolution (Bolshevism) around the First World War. Others take it back to the mid-19th century, promulgated by the ideology of Karl Marx (hence the frequently used expression "Cultural Marxism" as a parallel to the textbook term "Economic Marxism"). Still others see political correctness as a by-product of the turbulent social movements in the 1960s.

Whatever the origins, today's incoming freshmen in their orientation sessions will likely be given pre-set criteria for identifying select groups of people as "victims." The victimization can be based on real or imagined history. It does not matter. What does matter is that individual speech and behavior of the campus population must be modified so as to avoid *potentially* or *actually* offending these groups of "victims." Those victimized have become so well defined that their categories are ingrained within our social, economic, educational, and legal systems.

Much of our Western cultural heritage withers under the scrutiny of political correctness. Vast swaths of literature, art, music, dance, and particularly folklore, no matter how time-honored, now run the risk of being judged offensive to someone. Consequently, whole bodies of material, once hallowed, can no longer be taught in U.S. public schools and many universities. Classic poems, songs, paintings, monuments, and accounts of American history are being devalued or rewritten, if not repressed entirely.

Behind all of this ideological momentum lies the most feared word: litigation. Just the *threat* of lawsuits by the "offended" person or group is sufficient to plant terror in any responsible party, particularly faculty and administrators. So, schools, workplaces, and even churches have quickly snapped into a drastic phase of self-censorship.

The constant threat of litigation has distorted much that was admirable in our American system. Those who work in schools stay on the edge of paranoia. Outstanding teachers find themselves parsing through lecture notes to be sure their content does not "offend" anyone or contain phrases that will be misinterpreted. They drop illustrative stories they might have used freely in lectures not so long ago. They cull material out of their reading lists.

Now let me step back and say I fully acknowledge that many historical events *have* been vicious, bigoted, racist, and tragic. As someone who grew up in the South of the 1950s, I was appalled by things I witnessed. Beyond that, my own mother's family was decimated by the nightmare of pogroms in the late 19th century and the Holocaust in the 20th. So trust me, I know the evil forms that bigotry, prejudice, and hatred can take.

But redeeming the past is tricky business. Viewing past centuries through our 21st-century sensibilities is rarely productive. People must *understand* history rather than simplify the story into a set of hollow principles that can be easily used to repress once again.

So where does all of this leave today's students? My best advice is that they need first to make themselves aware of the politically correct prescriptions for what *not* to say. And it is best to learn these things before freshman orientation begins, rather than be blindsided by torrents of politically correct ideology. Sensitivity training, bias management, whatever the newest buzzwords might be, incoming freshmen are likely to hear them all.

After that, students can make their own decisions about whether or not they will follow those strictures, and in what situations. Discussions with parents and other trusted adults can help here and should make for lively dinner-table conversation.

It is true, though, that today's young people may be able to parse through and digest this ideology more easily than their parents or grandparents. Many students entering college have been raised (willingly or not) alongside the dogmas of political correctness. Just attending public school or watching any media has taught students the reasons why it is better to avoid expressing anything deemed potentially offensive. Still, teens must decide for themselves how to handle attacks on deeply held values.

So here are my strategies for helping students (and their families) prepare for, and survive, political correctness on campus.

    1. Remember you are going to college to get an education, not a political indoctrination, and you are probably paying a lot of money to obtain it! You are not there to be a crusader for any cause. It is fine to have well-formed opinions that you hold fervently, but do not be surprised when

others disagree just as fervently.

2. Educate yourself about the current ideological atmosphere on today's campuses and assess the degree to which your chosen campus is ruled by political correctness. Not all are, fortunately.

3. Pick your battles. Think through the ramifications before you broadcast opinions that clash with the easy-to-recognize tenets of political correctness. The old adage "There is a time and place for everything" can be a good guide.

4. Don't become embroiled in political correctness yourself by trying to take advantage of its ideologies to further your personal situation. In other words, if you decide to view yourself as a victim to obtain some special benefit, realize where that path may lead. Students obtaining a higher education at a good college or university are, by definition, not victims or suffering debilitating effects of past discrimination. They are among the luckiest and most blessed, enjoying benefits that most people across the world cannot obtain.

5. Learn to identify biases and ideological agendas in the texts, reading materials, and discussion questions for different classes.

6. Remember that most of your professors, for all their human quirks and imperfections, know something about their professional areas that you need to learn. Even if their ideas grate against yours, you need to pass the class. Keeping a professor's good will nearly always

matters, unless, of course, the situation is so aggressive that "good will" is impossible.

To summarize, try initially to talk less, and listen more. Listen to the general flow of conversation and analyze the directions it is taking. You are going to be studying and working with a new group of people, no matter where you attend school. Inevitably, that brings clashes of views (just as it will in your future workplaces).

Think first, speak second. Be open to hearing what people say, and try to understand other viewpoints. Work hard to analyze what you hear and read. Seek out a few like-minded friends with whom you *can* be honest in expressing yourself.

Finally, remember that truth endures and everything else passes. The social trends of today will pass. Into what direction, no one yet knows. Meanwhile, succeed in obtaining your education and then move into the next phase of your life!

CHAPTER 16

The Good News about Today's Colleges

After reading the previous chapters, teens (and their parents) may wonder, "Why would I even *want* to go to college?"

If you have the desire, the preparation, and a reasonable way to pay for it, then college may be a great choice for you. Today's campuses offer opportunities and resources unthinkable to students of previous generations. Once you learn to regulate your daily class and study schedule (remember the reasons freshmen fail in Part I), pick your friends *wisely*, and seek out good activities on campus, then you can have an excellent college experience.

Of course, the principal "good" result from college will be a student's education in a chosen field. But completing the credits in a degree program does not encompass or even reflect the spectrum of good things that can happen to a student who handles college wisely. So here are examples of the kinds of benefits that can accompany a college experience:

1. The easy availability of on-campus concerts, exhibits, and theatrical performances. Often free and incredibly convenient, these events require only that you walk from the dorm, show a student ID, and enjoy the event.

2. Options to study subjects not previously available to most high-school students, including courses in different languages and the Fine Arts.
3. The possibility of auditing (with permission) classes outside of your official degree requirements. Auditing a course (from the Latin *audire*, to hear) allows you to attend class meetings. You have to get permission from a professor to audit a course and may (or may not) have to do at least some of the class preparations. But you will not be required to take tests, nor will you receive a grade or credit. So you can focus strictly on learning.
4. The chance to participate in cultural and scholarly conferences, as well as professional gatherings of many kinds.
5. The possibility of hearing internationally renowned speakers who come to your campus on lecture tours.
6. Opportunities to attend religious services either on campus, or in neighboring churches or synagogues, thereby becoming connected to a supportive, new "spiritual family," even if far from home.
7. The availability of top-notch technological labs and facilities much harder to find, or afford, off campus. These may include art, dance, craft, or music studios open for all students to use.
8. A chance to meet and develop friendships with students from every part of the world.
9. The possibility of studying abroad for a semester

or year.

10. Regular opportunities to attend high-level competitive sporting events (often free), including sports such as rugby, crew, wrestling, table tennis, badminton, and track & field; also, options to use the excellent fitness facilities found in today's schools, as well as to participate in sports teams traditionally called intramural ("between the walls") available to all enrolled students.

I could mention more point-by-point benefits from enrollment in a college or university, but the listed items reinforce the idea that the years of college study can be broadly beneficial and set the tone for your entire future.

Young people, not surprisingly, tend to think of their impending college experience in pragmatic terms (go to University of XYZ, get a degree in computer programming, graduate, and find a high-paying job). Yet, the actual joy and personal benefit of a college education stem far more from the kinds of opportunities I have listed above. As life progresses, adults tend to look back on their college experiences with increasing fondness, especially if they took advantage of activities beyond the academic training. Never again does this period of life return for most people—a period where youthful enthusiasm meets up with boundless opportunities.

A student can forge lifelong friendships too in college, as well as business and social connections that can have far-reaching implications for the future. Plus, college sometimes can be the one time a person gets to live in a particular geographical location. For example, a teen from Boston will spend the college years in a small college in Iowa, or vice versa.

And speaking of small colleges, the advantages of a smaller campus are legendary: better student-to-professor ratios, more opportunities for leadership roles, and more ways to interact with the community at large. In addition, while large schools may have more sterling facilities and higher-profile events, smaller campuses often have the most wonderful traditions. Let me give you my favorite example.

My undergraduate institution, Hollins College (Virginia), was small—about a thousand students. An all-women's college replete with gorgeous antebellum architecture, Hollins lies nestled at the foot of Tinker Mountain in the Shenandoah Valley. Early one weekday each autumn, the college president makes a long-awaited announcement: "Today is Tinker Day." Students know this will happen, and they know a day will be picked that promises good weather. But which day is a surprise.

Students go to extremes to find out, including keeping watch to detect the kitchen staff baking cookies at 3 a.m. All told, the suspense and anticipation is half the fun. But when the announcement finally comes, classes are cancelled. Students gleefully trek up Tinker Mountain to find a sumptuous picnic awaiting them, as well as hours of games and songs.

Decades later, students who attended Hollins fondly recall the tradition of Tinker Day. Such traditions create bonds between students. They help define the identity of the school and, ultimately, the adult lives of those who graduate from the school.

Let me summarize: if the student handles the college years wisely, there are few better ways to achieve these kinds of academic and extra-curricular experiences, as well as gain interpersonal skills. The key, of course, is to handle the opportunities and responsibilities *well*.

So, if you make the decision to attend college, take seriously every chance to try new experiences that can stretch and enrich you. Partake of the time-honored traditions, even if they seem old-fashioned to you. Realize that *extra-curricular* activities will make you a deeper, better-balanced person. To your surprise, precisely these experiences may provide the ingredients in your professional profile that help you obtain interesting work or become a valuable member of your community and future family. Remember too, that each day at college, you are spending a fortune. Ordinarily, people do not openly choose to waste money. So do not waste your fortunate opportunity to attend a college or university—something that remains an impossible dream for many young people around the world.

CHAPTER 17

Are They Really Ready?

Throughout the high-school years, students pay so much attention to academic preparation, testing, and college applications, that they may not think to stop and ask a basic question: is going to college the best next step for me?

In our "go-go-go-to-college" culture, even posing this question could seem blasphemous to some (particularly to parents). "Of course my son is going to college!" a parent might say. Or we hear a mantra like this: "I went to college, his mother went to college, the grandparents went to college, his older siblings have gone to college . . . what else would he do?"

What else indeed! Before answering the "what else," consider four reasons why it is good to encourage students and their families to pose the question.

1. We are programmed in today's culture to believe that college is a superior choice for *everyone* after high school. But is it? Are there better options? What did people do in past decades, before the trendiness of a college education overwhelmed the marketplace?

2. College is an extremely expensive undertaking. Other than a house, a college education may be the biggest purchase in a person's lifetime. Even if students enroll in a government-subsidized community college or have a full scholarship,

there will be significant costs. Few things this expensive are automatically undertaken with so little scrutiny.

3. College study occupies four to five years of a young person's life. For someone aged eighteen, these are monumentally important years. College may be the right place to invest them. But spending time pursuing other options may better suit a student's abilities, and advance possibly better goals.

4. Eighteen-year-olds can convey more maturity than they possess. Behind a veneer of confidence lie inevitable doubts and insecurities. Even a teen who is a terrific student may sorely lack other skills (such as the workplace and interpersonal skills outlined in Part I). While college can help a student gain such confidence and skills, it is too expensive to be used primarily as a place to "grow up."

Now, as to the "what-else" question, take a look around our world. Who would have thought, a few decades ago, that students would be graduating in masses from expensive law schools and finding no jobs? Who would have foreseen a world where students race toward computer programming degrees, even if not particularly drawn to the field, because they believe (sometimes falsely) they will come out earning spectacular incomes?

Meanwhile, the world needs specialists of many other kinds. It has become a cliché to say, "Have you seen what plumbers make?" But is this not true? Anyone who has paid bills recently for construction, remodeling, or electrical services knows that the field of competent specialists is narrow and the financial rewards are great. I like to tell people that my son, after seven months of welding school following high school, began his career making more money than I did as a professor. Workers are needed in these fields, despite the society-induced "stigma" that learning trades and vocations is not as good as going to college. Among other things, the easy availability of loan money that turns into life-crushing debt has contributed to this misconception.

But beyond defending such practical options as a "what else" path for many young people, let's talk about something popularly known as a "gap year." A gap year allows a high-school graduate to engage in something completely different for a year, and then (perhaps) enter college with greater maturity and focus.

As a professor, I must tell you that my best students frequently had taken a gap year (whether they called it that or not). They had been out of school for some time—at least a semester or a year, and often longer. Some had served in the military; others worked for a year or two while saving money for college; still others spent significant time committed to some kind of mission or volunteer work. Each of these activities increased a young person's experience with the world outside of school. You can also find academic programs for gap years that build important skills—programs in classical education and writing skills, Great Books programs, foreign language institutes—that can significantly increase the likelihood of success in college.

On a personal level, a gap year would have benefited me enormously. By my senior year in high school, I had developed more interest in foreign languages and international affairs than in music. I might have used a "gap year" to decide to continue in music, as was expected, or to pursue a different education, such as becoming a translator or seeking a degree in international studies. Those would have been bold directions in my era, but they were possible. Yet my level of maturity did not allow me to ask these tough questions. And the momentum accumulating behind my years of musical training overwhelmed me. Without a chance to reflect, I basically plowed ahead. With a gap year, even if I had decided to stay with music studies, I am absolutely certain that most of the difficulties I experienced in college (described in Part I) would have vanished.

The main thing is, have the conversation. Put the question on the table: should this teen go to college? If so, why? What are the advantages? What are the trade-offs? What might happen if a period of time was taken before the decision, such as a gap year?

Don't be afraid to talk about this. In fact, don't be afraid of any of the conversations suggested in this book, from hashing through the thorny issue of political correctness to asking students if they really grasp how tempted they will be to skip classes. Now is the time to lay out the hard issues.

Here are sample approaches that parents might want to consider.

> *Look, Roland, I know you never skipped classes in high school and are extremely dependable. But the fact is, you always knew*

your mom and I were nearby, monitoring you. We won't be there, and you will have enormous pressures enticing you to all sorts of destructive behaviors, including missing classes, putting off your academic work, and far worse. People more disciplined than you have destroyed their college career by presuming they would never make these mistakes. Let's talk about how it happens, and what you're going to do about it.

Granted, Bethany, you had fabulous grades in high school. But we had to force you to do your homework and get projects done and turned in on time. Every morning it was a huge struggle just to get you up and ready for school. I want you to spend some time honestly considering whether more academic education, at this point of your life — this year — is what you really want. Or could there be some other kind of training or work that you're more interested in? Something that you would be more enthusiastic about? At least for right now?

Brooke, you aren't very comfortable with things that are different or unexpected in your life. But in college, you are going to be bombarded by different ideas and people, starting with having a roommate! So, between now and your high-school graduation, it might be good to find ways to get more exposure to new things and become more flexible and resourceful. Maybe that also will mean working for a semester before you go, doing some unusual volunteer work, or taking this summer and going abroad on [a mission trip, a study program].

Or, parents can take another approach. Sometimes students will write down what they are reluctant to say. So, put a piece of paper in front of the student and say, "Okay, write some answers for me. Here are the questions."

1. What are at least two reasons that you want to go to college? Do these reasons stand up under scrutiny? (Remember, this question came up in Chapter 3.)
2. Identify one or two things that have been difficult for you in high school. Do you think these things will become easier, or harder, in college? Why?
3. Are there paths you think about (career or personal) that interest you almost as much as college right now? If so, what are they? Why do they attract you?
4. Are you afraid that your family or your high-school teachers will be disappointed if you say you're not sure you want to go to college?
5. Are you worried that you will lose the opportunity to go to college if you delay college and pursue a different path for a bit (a gap year)?
6. What do you see yourself wanting to do in four years? In six years? In ten years?

Of course, if a young person has long dreamed of becoming a large-animal veterinarian, then the next step after high school may well be entering a college like Texas A&M and getting as quickly as possible into that major. But the next best step (for the sake of maturity and experience) could also be taking six months and working on a ranch or at a dairy.

Or, if a student is a terrific actor and intends to earn a degree in acting, then moving immediately to a university with a rigorous theater program may well be the best decision. But the student needs to be as eager to take that step as his high-school theater director might be. Talent in any field is a marvelous thing. But talent is not always a sufficient reason to pursue a particular professional direction. Parents or other mentors need to help a teen work through the options to make the best decision.

There are no guarantees in life. College, as a serious undertaking that occupies a critical time period in a young person's life, can be a magnificent experience. It can be a means to a desired end. It can change a life. But it must be approached with scrutiny, wisdom, and careful thought given to all the possibilities. The disadvantages need to be discussed openly and honestly. Particularly in this era where so many graduates are not finding jobs, cannot afford apartments or buy cars, and will have to spend two decades repaying student loans, the decision to go to college has to be undertaken with unprecedented seriousness. Once undertaken, the college experience needs to be approached with equal seriousness, employing every academic, spiritual, and practical skill a student possesses.

May the points that you have read in this book be helpful in your quest. Students, I encourage you to revisit these chapters periodically, particularly those in Part I. And may your next step after high school, no matter which direction you take, be fascinating, inspiring, and a blessing for you, your life, and for others whose lives you touch.

About the Author

Dr. Carol Reynolds weaves history, humor, and high energy into everything she does. She has toured since 2011 on behalf of Smithsonian as a speaker on numerous ocean and river cruises and as a study leader on Smithsonian tours throughout Eastern and Central Europe and in Russia.

A former professor of music history at Southern Methodist University in Dallas, Carol specializes in Russian Culture and German Romanticism. A native of Virginia, she received her bachelor's degree from Hollins College and her Ph.D. from the University of North Carolina at Chapel Hill. She is fluent in German and Russian.

Carol and her husband Hank have spent the past ten years on their small ranch in North Central Texas. Surrounded by goats, dogs, and cows, Carol spends her time at home designing multi-media Fine Arts curricula under the name "Professor Carol." Her unprecedented Discovering Music: 300 Years of Interaction in Western Music, Arts, History, and Culture (2009) has reached students across the world. She created additional courses in American Music, Russian Music and Culture, and the history of Sacred Music from Temple times through the Middle Ages.

Carol is a passionate advocate of Arts Education at every stage of life and can be found online at www.professorcarol.com.

Made in the USA
Monee, IL
21 June 2021